D1171827

LA
174
U5

Universities in politics; case studies from the late Middle **Ages** and early modern period. Edited with an introd. by John W. Baldwin and Richard A. Goldthwaite. Baltimore, Johns Hopkins Press ₁1972₎

137 p. 24 cm. (The Johns Hopkins symposia in comparative history, 2) $8.50

The Schouler Lectures for 1970, presented at Johns Hopkins University.
Includes bibliographical references.

1. Universities and colleges — History — Addresses, essays, lectures. 2. Higher education and state—Addresses, essays, lectures. I. Baldwin, John W., ed. II. Goldthwaite, Richard A., ed. III. Series.

LA174.U5   378.1'009   73–183041
ISBN 0–8018–1372–7   MARC

Library of Congress   72 ₍4₎   9 1

UNIVERSITIES IN POLITICS

THE JOHNS HOPKINS SYMPOSIA
IN COMPARATIVE HISTORY

The Johns Hopkins Symposia in Comparative History are occasional volumes sponsored by the Department of History at The Johns Hopkins University and The Johns Hopkins Press. Each considers, from a comparative perspective, an important topic of current historical interest and comprises original essays by leading scholars in the United States and other countries. The present volume is the second. Its preparation has been assisted by the James S. Schouler Lecture Fund.

UNIVERSITIES IN POLITICS

*Case Studies from the Late Middle Ages
and Early Modern Period*

Edited with an Introduction by

John W. Baldwin

and

Richard A. Goldthwaite

THE JOHNS HOPKINS PRESS

Baltimore and London

The Johns Hopkins Press, Baltimore, Maryland 21218
The Johns Hopkins Press Ltd., London

Library of Congress Catalog Card Number 73-183041
International Standard Book Number 0-8018-1372-7

Contents

JOHN W. BALDWIN

Introduction

On 11 May 1970 the Faculty of Arts and Sciences at The Johns Hopkins University voted overwhelmingly to suspend "classes for a two-week period prior to the fall elections to enable faculty members and students to campaign for congressional and senatorial candidates who will represent their views." This decision to enter the arena of politics taken on a balmy Friday afternoon marked a climax of events at Johns Hopkins not much different from what was unfolding on many American campuses during the spring of 1970. A few days earlier, in the wake of the Cambodian invasion, a university-wide referendum had brought about the suspension of military recruitment on the Hopkins campus by a narrow vote, but the feelings and decisions of the spring were not sustained through the following summer and fall. Late in the summer a student poll unequivocally rejected the faculty proposal to suspend classes for the November political campaign and supported retention of the normal academic calendar. Then late in September, when word was received of imminent congressional approval of a bill which would prohibit allocation of government funds to institutions of higher learning which barred the recruiting personnel of the armed forces, the Board of Trustees decided to abolish the restrictions against military recruiters on campus. The two major decisions taken during the spring were both reversed by fall. Thus ended a brief encounter with politics at The Johns Hopkins University.

1

In the spring of 1969, when the Department of History decided on "universities in politics" as the theme of the Schouler Lectures for 1970, it was certainly not unaware of its contemporary pertinence, but it did not anticipate that the lectures would be delivered amidst Johns Hopkins' own experiences in the politics of that year. (Mr. Christopher Hill's lecture took place one week before the faculty vote.) As observers of the contemporary scene, the members of the department realized that the problem of universities in politics would undoubtedly prompt polemicists of all political persuasions to look for historical origins and examples to support their rhetoric. But as professional historians themselves, they were naturally concerned that the historical aspects of the issue be treated by trained scholars rather than partisan myth-makers. To present historical case studies of the involvement of universities in politics, the Department chose a small group of major European universities. Four historians each of whom had devoted serious study to one of these universities, were invited to select an episode in which their university was called upon to play a role in politics during the Middle Ages or the Early Modern period. In order that these studies might stand as critical historical scholarship each lecturer was encouraged "to present his view of the past irrespective of its implications for today." Thus this volume contains four chapters on universities in politics: Dr. J. K. Hyde on Bologna during the communal period, M. Jacques Verger on Paris at the end of the Hundred Years' War, Professor Howard Kaminsky on Prague during the Hussite Revolution, and Mr. Christopher Hill on Oxford and Cambridge during the English Civil War. This preliminary introduction attempts to provide historical preparation and context for the four studies.

The modern university originated in the Middle Ages. It was not Aristotle's Lyceum at Athens or the Hellenistic Museum at Alexandria or the Muslim research institutes at Baghdad but the twelfth-century scholars of Bologna and Paris who first organized education in the form of a university. To appreciate the full extent of their achievement, its background should first be considered. When the ancient Roman world order succumbed to the pressures of internal dissolution and barbarian invasions in the fourth and fifth centuries, it bequeathed to the early Middle Ages political anarchy and economic stagnation. The chief victims of this general malaise were the cities, which shrank into the corners of their once-spacious walls. Since the ancient schools were usually located in urban centers, the classical educational system generally disappeared with municipal life. After this disintegration of the urban school system, except for a few areas bordering the Mediterranean, the tasks of learning were assumed by a new group of men, the monks. The sixth through the eleventh centuries may be rightfully called the monastic centuries of education.

Actually, the monastery was admirably suited to shelter the fruits of learning during the chaos of the early Middle Ages. Autocratically ruled by its abbot, it was independent of the prevailing political anarchy. Possessing large estates in the countryside, the monks attempted to be economically self-sufficient. Striving to achieve spiritual perfection, they were not only the spiritual elite of the clergy, the descendants of angels of earth, but they were largely recruited from the free classes and, later, from the noble elements of society. An aristocrat both spiritually and socially, independent economically, the monk of the early Middle Ages succeeded to the liberal professions of classical antiquity, which were formerly performed by free men of independent means. In this tradition monks took over the services of medicine and teaching, and monasteries provided hospitals and schools. The popular image of the solitary monk in his cell laboriously copying precious ancient manuscripts essentially captures the monastic contribution to education. Isolated in the countryside, monasteries performed a preservative function for education, defending the survivals of culture from an age in which illiteracy and barbarism predominated.

The eleventh and twelfth centuries witnessed an awakening of medieval society after a long epoch of chaos and stagnation. Population increased dramatically, agriculture became more productive, industry and commerce quickened, and, most important, urban life renewed its ancient vigor. Principally in Italy and northeast France, old Roman towns regained and exceeded their former dimensions, and new towns sprang up in response to the demands of expanding commerce. This urban revival also transformed the Church. The rural monks provided the Church with leadership in the early Middle Ages, but by the twelfth century the initiative had passed to a new urban clergy, the secular clergy. Termed secular because of their responsibility to minister to the outside world, these clergy contested the monks' right to preach, to administer the sacraments, and to collect tithes. Among these attempts to induce the monks to withdraw again from the world, the secular clergy attacked the monastic hospitals and schools. In 1163 the pope forbade monks to study law and medicine because these activities threatened their spiritual seclusion.

The monastic response to this opposition was to withdraw from education. Old monasteries began to reduce the size of their schools, and new orders such as the Cistercians abolished them from their constitutions. Schools began to appear in the churches of the secular clergy, principally in the cathedrals and collegiate churches of the north European towns. To encourage this movement the papacy required that each cathedral church support a resident teacher who would freely teach the rudiments of learning. Within these urban schools appeared the individual master who specialized and gained renown in a particular discipline. The numbers of these teachers grew in the early twelfth century: they included men such as Irnerius, who taught Roman law at Bologna, Gratian, who taught canon law at Bologna, and Abelard, who was pre-eminent in logic and theology at Paris. In an age of educational individualism the teaching of these masters was characterized by enthusiasm, informality, improvisation, and flux. But as these celebrated teachers succeeded in attracting more and more students, the need for control and protection of both students and teachers became increasingly evident. By the end of the twelfth century groups of academics had begun to organize themselves at Bologna and Paris, the former composed of students, the latter of masters. These two cities gave birth to a new educational regime, the university.

The Italian scene, of which Bologna was a part, provided some exceptions to the educational developments of western Europe. Because urban life in Italy did not suffer as severely as in the north and the upper elements of Italian society did not desert the towns as they did in the north, municipal schools persisted in Italy throughout the Middle Ages. The result of this survival was to reduce the clerical influence in education, both that of the monks and of the secular clergy, and to allow the laity a greater role in learning. This process is best seen in the emergence of the University of Bologna. Irnerius and Gratian, Bologna's renowned masters of the early twelfth century, specialized in legal studies, and their successors attracted large numbers of law students, who were predominantly laymen. Drawn from all over western Europe, these students were foreigners in a city where they needed essential rights and protection. As their numbers increased throughout the twelfth century, they were encouraged to organize for their mutual benefit.

In the first chapter of this book, J. K. Hyde describes in detail how the students' efforts to organize for mutual protection ran parallel to the Bolognese townsmen's attempts to form an association to defend the city against the endemic political anarchy of Italy produced by the absence of effective imperial authority. In short, the resultant Bolognese university and commune were simultaneous and similar efforts to provide security for their members. In particular, the University of Bologna formed a corporation fashioned after the closest example at hand, the urban craft and trade guilds. Like the guild, the Bolognese law students bound themselves with an oath, swore obedience to elected officials, and closely regulated admission to their membership. Because most professors were laymen and were dependent on student fees for their livelihood, the student university gained ascendancy over the teachers, and Bologna became the pre-eminent example of a student university. The commune of Bolognese citizens naturally regarded with suspicion the growing university of foreign students as potential rivals. Conflicts multiplied in the thirteenth century, but the students were able to defend their interests by going out on strike and migrating to other cities such as Vicenza, Arezzo, and Padua. Since university business was good business for the city of Bologna, the commune eventually permitted the student corporation its three basic requirements.

Just as Irnerius and Gratian inaugurated the emphasis on legal studies at Bologna, so Abelard and his successors attracted students and teachers to Paris who were devoted to the liberal arts and theology. But the university which emerged at the end of the twelfth century, unlike that at Bologna, was not composed of students but of masters. The reasons for this divergence are not fully apparent, but the fact that masters and students at Paris were members of the clergy seems significant. This clerical status endowed both teachers and pupils with protection and privileges not enjoyed by the lay students at Bologna. Furthermore, it provided some masters, although certainly not all, with regular ecclesiastical incomes which freed them from dependence on student fees. At Bologna most students were foreigners and most professors were citizens of the commune, but at Paris there were considerable numbers of foreigners among both masters and students. Protected by their ecclesiastical status, the clerical students at Paris had less incentive to organize and less control over their professors than their lay counterparts at Bologna. On the other hand, when organization for mutual protection was required, the masters assumed the leadership and were followed by their students. The capital of the French king and an important bishopric, the city of Paris was never permitted local self-government or a commune by its royal lord. When the university of masters began to demand self-determination early in the thirteenth century, it was contested not by a commune but by a church official, the chancellor of Notre-Dame, and by the Crown. As at Bologna, the university's chief weapons were the strike and migration, which were effectively brandished against the royal government from 1229 to 1231. In the ensuing struggle the masters received encouragement and support from the papacy. When the Crown finally conceded the masters' demands in 1231, the Pope solemnly confirmed the university's fundamental rights to organize as a sworn corporation and to strike. Championed by the papacy, the University of Paris achieved independence based on its corporate privileges.

Bologna and Paris, therefore, set the pattern for universities throughout western Europe. Italian universities such as Padua and legal universities such as Orléans in France followed Bologna's example of student organization. But the Paris solution was adopted by the northern European universities, of which Oxford, Cambridge, and Prague were illustrious examples.

In contrast to the monastic centuries of education, the schools and universities of the twelfth and thirteenth centuries produced a veritable revolution. Unlike the old monasteries in their rural isolation, the schools and universities were an integral part of the new urbanism. The crowded, bustling, energetic atmosphere of the town formed the habitat of the scholar. While the former teacher was rooted to his cell—a monk out of his cell is like a fish out of water, so ran the monastic adage—the new masters and teachers were ever on the move. Abelard transported his school from Paris to Melun and throughout the Champagne countryside, followed by a clamoring band of devoted pupils. While the monk was careful to seclude himself from the confusion of the sinful world, the new masters opened their classrooms to a larger society. Following a long history of municipal and lay education in Italy, the schools of Bologna invited large numbers of laymen to study law. In the north the secular clergy, whose primary responsibility was to minister to the world, assumed the tasks of instruction. Later in the thirteenth century the universities attracted the new mendicant orders, such as the Dominicans and Franciscans, whose prime mission was to prepare themselves for preaching to the urban masses. From their number the Dominican Thomas Aquinas and the Franciscan Bonaventure were pre-eminent among the professors of the University of Paris. While the monastic ideal was inner quiet and harmony of soul, the university master lived in a world of contention and conflict both within his school and without. In his classroom one of the principal modes of instruction was the disputation, in which all problems were susceptible to arduous debate and which at times degenerated into less edifying brawls. In the outside world he was constantly defending his privileges and rights against the encroachments of Church officials, communes, and royal authority.

The underlying characteristic which distinguished the medieval university from all previous educational regimes was its corporatism. Unlike the monastic scholar, who often studied in isolation, the university masters and students invariably worked as a group. Following the pattern of the trade and craft guild, they sought to organize themselves for the regulation of the conditions vital to their profession. Chief among these was exclusive admission to membership, and the universities guarded this privilege with hypersensitivity. At Paris the stages of academic advancement closely corresponded to the hierarchy of the guilds. At the bottom were the ordinary students, equivalent to the guild apprentices who were learning the elements of the trade and were under the full authority of the master craftsmen. Next came the bachelors, who were advanced students and were allowed to lecture and dispute under supervision. They corresponded to and derived their names from the journeymen or bachelors, who worked for a daily wage and had not sufficient maturity to establish themselves in the trade. (Hence they were still unmarried.) At the top of the profession was the master, a rank common to both universities and guilds. He was a man who had demonstrated both his skill and maturity to the satisfaction of his fellow masters. Entrance to this stage was gained after elaborate examinations, exercises in the techniques of teaching, and ceremonial investiture. Admission fell exclusively under the jurisdiction of the other full members of the university. Of course, at Bologna, where the corporation was composed of students, membership qualifications in the university were of a different order than at Paris. But these members, whether they were masters at Paris or students at Bologna, bound themselves with an oath to obey their elected officials. At their head was a rector, whose very title was borrowed from guild terminology. Under his leadership the university exercised its principal defensive maneuvers, mentioned above—the strike, the cessation of activities, and the migration to other localities. The great migrations from Bologna to Padua in 1222 and from Paris to various other cities in 1229 were highly effective in obtaining those rights and privileges deemed essential by the universities.

North of the Alps the universities were not only corporate bodies but were also predominantly clerical. The close assimilation of their members with the clergy provided both masters and students with valuable privileges and protection. As a clergyman the scholar's person was regarded as sacred, and any physical abuse was regarded as sacrilege, punishable by severe penance and spiritual disabilities. Even in the crude conduct of the Middle Ages one thought twice before striking a cleric. Moreover, all clergy were subject to the exclusive jurisdiction of the Church courts and could not be punished by the secular police or judges. Since the ecclesiastical courts were prohibited from meting out corporal punishments, a scholar found added advantage in his clerical status. As members of the clergy and eligible for benefices or income drawn from churches, many students and masters (although certainly not all) could not support themselves through their ecclesiastical positions. If they were not so fortunate to possess a benefice, they nonetheless claimed the right as clerics to ask for alms and donations from all men of good will. Clerical membership, therefore, was a substantial factor in the economic condition of the scholars of the north. Even in Italy, where lay conditions predominated, the clerical element was not altogether absent. The canon lawyers at Bologna, for example, were largely recruited from the clergy, and, according to the imperial privilege, the *Authentica Habita*, issued by Emperor Frederick Barbarossa in 1158, the lay students of Bologna had the right to refuse the secular courts in favor of trial under the jurisdiction of their masters or in the Church courts of the bishop. Whether clerical or not, the scholar occupied a privileged position in medieval society. But, as would be expected, the clerical orientation of the northern university gave a religious cast to all of its interests. The theological faculty at Paris considered itself an unimpeachable authority in all questions involving the Christian religion. Those universities such as Oxford, Cambridge, and Prague which were modeled on its organization also asserted their expertise in religious matters.

Despite the clerical organization of the northern universities the scholar of the High Middle Ages rejected the monastic traditions for a new exemplar, the townsman. Like the urban merchant, he traveled far and wide in search of the most profitable intellectual wares. Like the urban artisan, he worked in a classroom shop with the cooperation of his apprenticed students. As we have seen, he organized his profession along the lines of the contemporary guilds. Perhaps most indicative of this transformation of the scholarly image was an important change in the economics of learning which broke with ancient tradition. Inspired by the example of Socrates, the liberal professions of classical antiquity evoked the ideal of rendering services as an act of friendship and refusing to accept direct remuneration. Since the monastic teachers received their support directly from the monasteries in the early Middle Ages, they too were able to dispense their services gratuitously. But in the twelfth and thirteenth centuries, when the numbers of masters and students rose sharply, the supply of church benefices was insufficient for the clerical teachers of the north and was unavailable to the lay teachers of the south. To finance the growing universities a new economic basis was devised, the academic fee, by which the master charged his students directly for his instruction. Like the urban artisan, the master fashioned his intellectual wares in the atelier of his classroom and sold them to his students at a price to compensate his skill and labor. This academic fee exemplified the final urbanization of the university profession.

The Middle Ages witnessed not only the appearance of the university but also the emergence of the modern state. Government by commune, such as arose at Bologna, originated among the Italian cities in the eleventh and twelfth centuries and from there spread among the prospering cities of northwest Europe. But this communal organization, resembling that of a university, was suitable only for local government and could not cope with the problems of substantially extended areas. In response to the national aspirations of large populations, territorial monarchies appeared, first in England and then in France, in the twelfth and thirteenth centuries. The Plantagenet kings of England, followed by the Capetian kings of France, created monarchical and territorial forms of government which extended far beyond the local communities. The Salian and Hohenstaufen imperial dynasties experimented with similar designs for Germany and Italy but failed in the thirteenth century, when the English and French kings were consolidating their authority. It was unavoidable that these new monarchs would perceive the value of flourishing schools and universities in their realms and would enlist the help of the scholar in achieving their political purposes. At the beginning of the twelfth century Emperor Henry V consulted frequently with the Bolognese scholar Irnerius; Emperor Frederick Barbarossa drew up the important provisions of the Diet of Roncaglia in 1158 with the aid of four law professors from Bologna who were Irnerius's students. In 1169 King Henry II was willing to resolve his dispute with Archbishop Thomas Becket according to the arbitration of the masters of Paris. Opportunities for political consultation and influence increased as universities grew in prestige throughout the Middle Ages, but it was the upheavals of the fifteenth century that present us with the two most striking case studies of universities in politics: Paris during the Hundred Years' War and Prague during the Hussite Revolution.

Throughout the thirteenth century the University of Paris enjoyed the solicitous patronage of the papacy. At the end of the century, when Pope Boniface VIII opposed the achievement of the nationalistic goals of the French monarch, Philip the Fair, the king began to supplant the pope as the chief protector of the masters of Paris. By the middle of the fourteenth century King Charles V had accorded to the university the title of "the eldest daughter of the king of France," which signified its increased dependence on the Crown. But the Hundred Years' War dealt the Valois dynasty heavy blows and thus provided new opportunities for the university to regain its independence and play

an influential role in French politics. In the second chapter of
this volume Jacques Verger recounts the political activities of
the University of Paris at the conclusion of the Hundred Years'
War and analyzes the goals and failings of the Parisian scholars
in politics. Obsessed with the defense of their own privileges and
entranced by the outmoded ideal of a universal Christendom,
the masters of Paris ignored the currents of contemporary
nationalistic feeling and therefore failed to offer realistic political
advice. Oscillating in support of the English, the Burgundians,
and the dual monarchy, and finally returning to back the restored Valois, the university emerged even more dependent than
ever on its royal lords.

When Emperor Charles IV founded the University of Prague
in 1348, the first university east of the Rhine and north of the
Alps, he had Paris in mind as his exemplar. Not only did the
university consist of a corporation of masters but, like Paris, it
was religious in orientation and international in outlook. The
most prestigious masters and the majority of students were drawn
from the German lands, which had long been deprived of any
university. At the beginning of the fifteenth century, however,
Prague became the scene of the Hussite Revolution, which was
both nationalistic and religious in purpose. In the third chapter
of this book, Howard Kaminsky describes the part played by
the university masters during the upheavals. Unlike their
Parisian contemporaries, the Czech masters were responsive to
the nationalistic striving of their countrymen, but they ignored
the popular religious fervor of the Taborite movement. As a
result of this blind spot, the activity of the university was brought
to a virtual standstill. Thus in these two experiments in political
action the universities of Paris and Prague failed to assess their
goals realistically and to act effectively.

The weight of long years of royal pressure at Paris eventually
dissolved the corporate structure of the university there. By the
sixteenth century Paris had gone from a closely knit, self-
conscious guild of masters to a loose aggregate of colleges which
had lost its collective purpose. The college at its inception in the
twelfth century was a charitable foundation to provide lodging

and food for poor scholars. As colleges attracted rich benefac-
tions and multiplied, they not only supported students but also
drew in masters, who began to hold classes under their roofs. By
the late Middle Ages most instruction at Paris took place within
the collegiate precincts, and the corporate faculty had been
scattered among the individual colleges.

We find the English universities of Oxford and Cambridge at
this stage of development in the seventeenth century. Emerging
as societies of masters like Paris and closely following the
development of their French exemplar in the Middle Ages, in
the sixteenth century they too felt the heavy hand of royal
despotism, that of the Tudor dynasty. During this period both
the royalty and the aristocracy lavished rich gifts on the Oxford
and Cambridge colleges, which eventually displaced the old
medieval halls as the principal residences for students. Because
of heavy dependence on their patrons, more and more of the
colleges were headed by men directly appointed by the Crown.
By the seventeenth century the governance of the English universities had passed from the corporation of masters to an
oligarchic council composed principally of the heads of colleges
who were dependent on royal favor. In 1604 King James I
graciously bestowed on the two universities the right to send
two members each to Parliament to represent their interests. In
the practical politics of the seventeenth century, however, these
university representatives were of little consequence. Considered
primarily as safe seats for the Crown, they devoted most of their
attention to protecting the particular interests of their con-
stituencies. Oxford and Cambridge took surprisingly little part
in the ferment and revolution which convulsed English society
in the seventeenth century. Corporate solidarity among the
masters gave way to individual opinion as the chief channel of
expression. Therefore, when Christopher Hill investigates the
role of Oxford and Cambridge in the Puritan Revolution in the
fourth chapter of this book, he focuses on individual critics such
as William Dell, Master of Gonville and Caius College at Cambridge, and Gerrard Winstanley, the Digger, a complete outsider.
These radical critics sought to disassociate the universities from

the contemporary social structure, which, in their view, meant the Church, a clerical orientation, and support of tithes. But their proposals to secularize, laicize, make more scientific, and multiply the universities of their day went unheeded, and Oxford and Cambridge were unreformed until the nineteenth century.

In the failures depicted by these case studies of universities in politics, a few common themes become apparent. Throughout all runs a propensity on the part of university scholars to theoretical abstraction and a failure to profit from concrete analysis and realistic observation. Elaborating Roman law as an academic text, the legists at Bologna found little application of their jurisprudence to the formation of the commune and university of their day. During the Hundred Years' War the masters of Paris were inclined to regard war as an absolute evil and peace an absolute good, a bias which blinded them to politically feasible solutions. Still defending the traditional ideal of a universal Christendom, they refused to acknowledge the nationalistic and secular factors which were animating their world. Although the Prague masters' espousal of Wyclifean political religion supported contemporary Bohemian aspirations for national independence, the academics still misjudged the force of popular religious conviction expressed in the Taborite movement and thereby destroyed the university. The reforms proposed by Dell and Winstanley to secularize the English universities thoroughly were too radical to receive widespread attention.

Perhaps more important than this lack of realism, however, was the inability of the universities to extricate themselves from the prevailing social structure. The clerical garb bequeathed by the University of Paris was a garment too comfortable to be shed by the northern universities. As late as the fifteenth century the Paris masters were unable to conceive of existence without their ecclesiastical privileges and their Church benefices. At the same time the Bohemian masters coveted the prebends of the foreign masters at Prague. Even in the seventeenth century Oxford and Cambridge retained their dominant function as schools for the clergy, and university instruction depended heavily on income from ecclesiastical tithes. Not only tied to the Church, but tied to it in an age when the Church was more and more the servant of the king, the universities could not escape the force of politics. In the end the masters of Prague became the spokesmen for the Czech nobility, and at Paris, Oxford, and Cambridge, where royal sovereignty was supreme, the universities had little other choice than to submit. In these case studies the story of the university's entry into politics becomes that of the domination of the university by politics.

J. K. HYDE

1 | Commune, University, and Society in Early Medieval Bologna

Communes and universities have a good claim to be considered the two most significant institutions left to the modern world by the Middle Ages. The medieval legacy in the form of national monarchies and parliaments is generally given greater prominence because it is forgotten that these eventually prevailed only in certain parts of Europe; outside the British Isles, the links between the modern state and democracy and their medieval counterpart are tenuous or nonexistent. The institutions of civic government and higher education have also been transformed and adapted almost out of all recognition, yet some kind of continuity from medieval times has been preserved in many parts of the Continent, and the words commune and university still carry overtones of independence and government by consultation which can be traced to their medieval roots.

Both communes and universities arose spontaneously as a response to the anarchy and confusion of the early Middle Ages and took on their definitive form in the crucial period of the last decades of the twelfth century and the first years of the thirteenth. There are many striking parallels between them. Both existed in distinct northern and southern types, the former more hierarchical and disciplined, the latter more libertarian and democratic. This was because in the north the communes and universities were implanted in societies where territorial monarchies and principalities were also evolving, while in the southern area city-states became the prevailing political institution with whom the universities, formed in a similar republican image and likeness, had to learn to live. The protoype of the northern universities, Paris, took shape in a city without a commune, and both city and university flourished under the paternal protection of the French Crown; Bologna, the premier university of the southern type, was, as Carducci said, the university of the Italian communes *par excellence*, with its home in one of the most turbulent and democratic of the city-states.

Much has been written about the origins and early development of both the Italian communes and universities.[1] The aim of the present chapter is not to add to this body of knowledge and theory, but through the outstanding example of Bologna, to look at the two institutions together in the setting of the distinctive society which gave them birth. Our concern will be not so much with the disputes between the commune and the university as with the underlying parallels in their development which may be discerned even when evidence for direct contact between them is lacking. What the sources of the period present resembles a double line of stepping stones, one for the commune and another for the university, occasionally linked by a bank of gravel but generally divided by the dark stream of our igno-

---

[1] Prevalent views on the Italian communes derive from those of G. Volpe, which are most concisely expressed in his volume of essays *Medioevo italiano*, 2d ed. (Florence, 1961), especially pp. 85–232. See also N. Ottokar, "Il problema della formazione comunale," in *Questioni di storia medioevale*, ed. E. Rota (Milan, n.d.), and G. Fasoli, *Dalla «civitas» al comune nell'Italia settentrionale* (Bologna, 1969), among many others. On the universities, the classic studies of H. S. Denifle (*Die Entstehung der Universitäten des Mittelalters* [Berlin, 1885]) and H. Rashdall (*The Universities of Europe in the Middle Ages*, 2 vols., ed. F. M. Powicke and A. B. Emden [Oxford, 1936]) are still fundamental. For Bologna, the series *Studi e memorie per la storia dell'università di Bologna* (hereafter cited as *Studi*), published by the Istituto per la storia dell'università di Bologna from 1907 on, contains many articles of value, especially the first volume of the new series (1956), in which the study "«Universitas scholarium» e comune," pp. 173–266, by G. Rossi, is particularly relevant to the present theme. Noteworthy is S. Stelling-Michaud, *L'Université de Bologne et la pénétration des droits romain et canonique en Suisse au XIIIe et XIVe siècles* (Geneva, 1955), which provides an admirable short introduction to the beginnings and early development of legal studies at Bologna. G. Cencetti, "Studium fuit Bononie," *Studi medievali* 7, no. 2 (1966): 781–833, surveys the main points of controversy.

rance. The present survey aims to throw some light on the nature of the river bed of Italian society on which the commune, the university, and the contacts between them all rested.

To carry out this purpose, it will be necessary to devote the greater part of this chapter to a period when one of its subjects, namely, the university, did not yet exist, for the commune and the university were not twins. In a strict sense, the University of Bologna did not emerge until the turn of the thirteenth century, almost exactly a hundred years after the formation of the commune. Consequently, for the first century of its development, the counterpart of the commune in the academic sphere must be sought in the schools of law and rhetoric from which the university finally evolved. The devotion of so much space to the pre-university period in a volume dedicated to universities and politics perhaps calls for some justification. The danger of such a theme is that it may suggest a false dichotomy between the worlds of learning and of politics, based on an underestimation of the social links between them. This illusion is easier to sustain in considering periods when both states and institutions of learning had well-defined constitutions. By looking first at a time when both worlds were still in a state of flux, the reader may be reminded that neither academics nor politicians work in isolation, but both are rooted in society—in this case, the cramped, violent, and competitive society of medieval Bologna.

The Emergence of the Bolognese Law School
in Its Contemporary Background

Being primarily concerned with useful knowledge such as theology and canon law, which would enable their devotees to get on in the Church and in the hereafter, and with medicine and secular law, which would help man's lot in the present world, the medieval universities paid little attention to history, even their own, so that for what may be called the "authorized version" of the foundation of the Bolognese law school it is customary to turn to the jurist Odofredo, who flourished in the middle of the thirteenth century. From incidental remarks in his lectures, it is possible to piece together the following story.[2] Originally, the *studium* of law was in Rome, but during a period of war "in the Marches" the school and the books of law were transferred to Ravenna, "where Charles set up his abode." Following the death of Charles, this city fell into decay. Eventually, a certain Pepo began on his own authority to teach law in Bologna, but whatever degree of learning he attained, it seems that by Odofredo's time all knowledge of his teaching had perished. Then came Irnerius, originally a master of arts in Bologna, who took up the study of the law on his own and made the first glosses, some of which were, in Odofredo's view, more obscure than the texts they were supposed to explain. He began the process by which the whole of Justinian's *Corpus* was brought to light, and he enjoyed a great reputation. Thus he became the founder of the Bolognese school, the lantern of the law and the illuminator of the science of jurisprudence.

This traditional account, recorded something like a hundred and fifty years after the events described, can only be regarded as myth, that is, as a justification in historical terms of the state of affairs as it existed in the thirteenth century. Like all myth, it floats in time without any anchor in exact chronology, so that some scholars have seen the reference to wars near Rome as referring to the sack by the Normans in 1084, though when the story is considered as a whole, it seems much more likely that the Gothic and Lombard invasions of the sixth century are meant. What the myth does make plain is that the Bolognese tradition of the thirteenth century regarded the study of Roman law as something which should be linked to the seat of an imperial administration; the association of Charlemagne with the transfer to Ravenna makes this point clear. Fortunately, this part of the tradition can be securely traced back to the twelfth century, for in a gloss by Pilleo da Medicina which dates from the 1170s or 1180s there is an earlier and historically more accurate account which attributes the decline of the imperial

[2] N. Tamassia, "Odofredo: Studio storico-giuridico," *Atti e memorie della deputazione di storia patria per la Romagna* (hereafter cited as *AMDSP*) 3, no. 12 (1895): 41–42.

schools of Rome and Constantinople to the schism within the Empire "in modern times." As a result of this rift, law came to be taught in various places, but chiefly in Bologna, which came to hold the primacy (*monarchiam*) in legal studies.[3] Given the imperial bias in the tradition, the fact that neither imperial foundation nor authorization is alleged for the Bologna school takes on great significance. Pilleo saw Bologna's pre-eminence as essentially fortuitous; indeed, as he wrote, he probably hoped that this primacy was about to pass to Modena, where he happened to be teaching himself at the time. This would have been anathema to Odofredo as a loyal Bolognese, but his choice of words indicates that he supports Pilleo on the essentially spontaneous nature of the Bolognese revival: he says Pepo took up the study of the law "*auctoritate sua*" and, of Irnerius, "*studuit per se sicut potuit*"—he studied on his own as best he might. This admission is the more significant since in other places Odofredo retails a later tradition which attributed the legalization, though not the foundation, of the Bolognese school to an act of the Emperor Theodosius.[4] Clearly these two stories existed in separate compartments of Odofredo's mind, and it had not yet occurred to him that they needed to be reconciled.

There is little doubt that the Bolognese law school owed its origin to the initiative of one or two private individuals, masters of arts such as were to be found in many Italian cities in the later eleventh century, who turned to the study of Roman law on their own account. Irnerius succeeded, through the excellence of his teaching, in establishing a reputation for the Bologna school, which spread rapidly first in Italy and then throughout Latin Christendom.[5] The local social and political setting in which this was achieved is obscure, but enough is known to show that it was one of unusual instability and upheaval. It can be briefly characterized as a time when in the cities of northern Italy a political system of great antiquity was on the point of

[3] Cited by Azzo, *Summa codicis* III. 19.
[4] See below, p. 44.
[5] As early as the 1120s a poet of Como wrote of *docta Bononia cum legibus suis*: Anon. Comensis, *De bello Mediolanensium adversus Comenses*, RIS [Rerum Italicarum Scriptores], vol. 5, p. 453.

collapse, while a new one was reaching out uncertainly to take its place. The old régime was essentially that of the late Christian Roman Empire of Diocletian, Constantine, and Justinian, scarred and distorted by centuries of barbarian onslaught and control.[6] To the end, however, it retained the characteristic marks of its late Roman origin—a high degree of centralization and territorialization. The prince, whether he was the Roman emperor of east or west or the king of Lombardy or of the *Regnum Italicum* founded by the Carolingians, was regarded as the fount of all authority with a theoretical right to intervene in government at every level. He was supposed to be served by a hierarchy of officials whom he directly appointed and dismissed, most of whom were responsible for defined territorial areas, notably the provinces which had been swept away by the barbarian invasions, but which had been replaced to some degree by the Carolingian marches, and the city-regions, properly called *civitates*. These had long ago lost their assemblies of local notables or *curiae*, and the prince's local representatives were supposed to be the count and bishop, though by the eleventh century long periods of inadequate supervision had produced a situation in which the secular power of one or the other, if not both, was in eclipse. In the major cities there was generally a royal palace to which corporations of administrators, merchants, and trades-men—the latter known as *ministeria*—were attached. The best evidence for the system of *ministeria*, or guilds under the control of royal officials, pertains to Pavia, which was unique in that it was the ancient capital of the Italian kingdom, so that the tolls collected along the entire northern frontier of the realm had been assigned to the maintenance of the palace there.[7] Char-acteristically, these rights were regarded as attached to the palace itself, regardless of whether it was the effective seat of

[6] A. H. M. Jones, *The Later Roman Empire* (Oxford, 1964), is an up-to-date guide to Roman administration; the standard textbooks to Dark Age Italy are G. Romano and A. Solmi, *Le dominazioni barbariche in Italia*, 2 vols. (Milan, 1940–45), and C. G. Mor, *L'età feudale* (Milan, 1952).

[7] The *Honorancie civitatis papie* is published in Monumenta Germaniae His-torica, scriptores 30, no. 2, pp. 1444–60, and again with full discussion in A. Solmi, *L'amministrazione finanziaria del regno italico nell'alto medioevo* (Pavia, 1932).

the royal administration or not; so that the disgruntled Pavian to whom we owe our information was still laying claim to them soon after 1024, although the palace had not been used as a royal residence for any length of time since the accession of the Saxon emperors in 962.

When Irnerius was growing up in Bologna every part of this ancient system was under great strain, if not actually breaking down. There was still a Roman emperor, but since 962 he had been a German and generally an absentee and from 1076 onward he was in violent conflict with the other pillar of world government, the pope. The Investiture Contest split the old order from top to bottom, dividing the nobles and prelates on whose shoulders it rested into two hostile camps, while the issue of Church reform inspired the new classes of citizens—and even the urban mob—to take a hand in political affairs. The struggle between pope and emperor brought a trail of disruption and civil war to Bologna, as to many other cities. In the imperial system, the counts of Bologna were subordinates of the archbishops of Ravenna, whose postion as imperial representatives in a wide area of northeastern Italy had been built up by successive emperors during the eleventh century.[8] When Archbishop Wibert of Ravenna became the imperialist anti-pope after Henry IV's break with Gregory VII, it became likely that discontent in the area would crystallize around the cause of the papacy and Church reform. This was especially true in the region of Bologna, which was partly encircled by the territory of the great Countess of Tuscany, Matilda, one of the greatest secular champions of the papacy in Italy. At first Bologna remained faithful to Henry IV, but the Church within the city was split, and by 1096 it had come over to the papal side. It may have been about this time that the royal palace in Bologna came under the control of Matilda, but proof is lacking; the power of the count was in eclipse, and the bishops of Bologna never exercised comital powers in the city.

In a situation which must often have lapsed into anarchy,

[8] A. Hessel, *Geschichte der Stadt Bologna* (Berlin, 1910), pp. 22f.

those in a position to do so banded themselves together for their mutual protection without reference to higher authority, and thereby created the institutions of the future. From the time of the Lombard invasions, groups of kinsmen had banded together for the defense of their members through the common pursuit of the vendetta. In the eleventh century these associations received a new lease of life among the nobility with the formation of tower societies, in which one or more clans joined together to provide for their common defense in town or country.[9] Another form of association for which there is a thin trickle of evidence in the eleventh and twelfth centuries is the confraternity by which men bound themselves together for religious and social benefits on the basis of common residence or trade and common worship at a particular church or altar. From Ferrara there is an example of a religious confraternity which shows no evidence of any trade associations or functions in 1112 but which, by the end of the century, had become a guild of shoemakers, regulating the practice of the trade under the patronage of a leading member of the citizen body.[10]

The commune was the most important form of association which emerged in this crisis; it was neither a tower society nor a confraternity, but it had some of the characteristics of each. It was essentially a spontaneous creation of local initiative, a response of the powerful men of a city or neighborhood to the collapse of the old order. It consisted of a number of individuals who bound themselves together by an oath of mutual support and common obedience to elected officials and who together were strong enough to take over virtual control of the area from what was left of the older organs of government, generally without much of a struggle. But although they included members of the old governing classes, such as counts and the feudal knights with whom the bishops had been accustomed to share their

[9] An arbitration by Archbishop Daimbert of Pisa (1088–92) includes provisions limiting the height of towers: F. Bonaini, *Statuti inediti della città di Pisa* (Florence, 1854–57), vol. 1, pp. 16–18.

[10] L. Simeoni, "Il documento ferrarese del 1112 della fondazione dell'arte dei calegardi," *Rendiconto dell'Accademia di Scienze di Bologna* 3, no. 7 (1932): 56–71.

secular power, the commune did not evolve out of the institutions of the old régime. Whether it was violent or bloodless, the formation of the communes marked an essentially new departure. Its characteristics provide a marked contrast with those of the old order. The authority of its officials, first known as *boni homines* and later as consuls, came from below, from the members of the association, and not hierarchically from above, as it had generally done under the old régime.[11] Furthermore, the commune was personal, providing first and foremost for the defense of the common interests of its members and only gradually taking over public responsibility within a defined territory. The initiative came from a minority of the inhabitants, who soon took it upon themselves to speak in the name of the whole community, on occasion strengthening their authority by having their decisions acclaimed by the old customary assembly of all the inhabitants, known as the *concio* or *parlamentum*. Despite this tendency toward identification with the city, the commune retained traces of its unofficial orgins. If the Genoese commune, known locally as the *compagna*, was at all typical, the commune was a temporary institution, formed for a fixed term of years and lapsing if not renewed at the end of that time. Again, there are signs that a commune could be mobile, not only in the case of the ports of Genoa and Pisa, where overseas expeditions seem to have been regarded as the commune on the move, but also on occasions when the armies of inland cities on campaign held assemblies and even passed legislation in camp or on the field exactly as if they were in the customary meetingplace within the city walls.[12] The contrast with the rigid centralization and territorialization of the old régime could hardly be more pronounced.

[11] The great exception being the bishop, who, as the Milanese chronicles show, in the eleventh century was still likely to be the nominee of the local notables.

[12] For Pisa and Genoa, see Volpe, *Medioevo italiano*, pp. 197f. Examples of inland cities: the Council of Modena meets in the bishop's tent outside the castle of Bazzano, September 1211 (L. V. Savioli, *Annali bolognesi* [Bassano, 1784], vol. 2, pt. 2, doc. 397); the Bolognese general and special council meet in camp outside Imola, *sonitu tubarum et voce preconia*, May 1248 (Archivio di Stato, Bologna, Registro grosso, fol. 2).

Bolognese Jurists, Roman Law, and the Medieval Empire

It was precisely in the years when the old order was breaking down in Bologna, and the first stirrings of the commune may have been heard in the streets, that Irnerius must have turned from the teaching of the liberal arts to the intensive study of the *Corpus iuris civilis*. What he and his pupils found must have been quite unlike anything they had ever known: there was the whole of the old imperial system of law and government, together with much of the philosophy which had inspired it, preserved in great detail and apparent orderliness through the work of Justinian's team of codifiers, who in codifying had been able to record the ideal without the necessity of taking into account the degree to which it was realized in practice. That the text was in places difficult to understand only added to the excitement of the discovery. The contrast between the brave old world of Justinian and the tattered society in which they lived was sufficient to inspire generation after generation of students at Bologna and elsewhere to study, explain, and comment, until at last, after Bartolo and Baldo, in about the middle of the fourteenth century, the game of reconciling the contemporary world and its institutions to the ideal of Justinian began to lose some of its fascination. The fact that the academic study of Roman law began in Bologna at the very time when the system of government based upon it was breaking down there is not so paradoxical as it might seem, for it was the "otherness" of the *Corpus iuris civilis* which provided the challenge and the intellectual stimulus. The particular mark of the early Bolognese school seems to have been a rigorously academic approach which sought to understand the texts in their own right before seeking practical applications, as compared, for example, to the more utilitarian attitude shown by the jurists of Pisa. The Bolognese believed in the practical application of their knowledge, but they seem to have distinguished between the role of the doctor, which was to explain and elucidate the text, and that of the judge or lawgiver, which was to apply the principles derived from academic study to a particular situation.

There were, however, certain conflicts between the texts of the *Corpus iuris civilis* and medieval practice which were too fundamental to be ignored. Here I would like to examine briefly those involving law schools, corporations, and the relationship between civic statutes and the common law, which have a special relevance for the development of both the commune and the university. In the constitution *Omnem* which provides an introduction to the Digest, Justinian had laid down that the law was to be taught only in the "royal" cities of Rome and Constantinople and, by special concession, also in Berytus. Those who presumed to teach elsewhere, like the inexpert men at Caesaria and Alexandria, of whom the Emperor had heard, were threatened with a fine and expulsion from the cities in which "they have not taught but rather violated the law."[13] This typical piece of late Roman centralization posed a serious problem for the Bolognese jurists. A historical interpretation was—with a very few exceptions—beyond them. The general view was that the Roman Empire still existed and that, in default of any more recent legislation on the subject, the law of the *Corpus* ought still to apply. For well over a century, the Bolognese school lived with the paradox that the text it taught prohibited its own existence and it was not until the early thirteenth century that a solution was found in a very forced interpretation of a historical legend which was held to prove that Bologna had been designated a *civitas regia* by Emperor Theodosius.[14]

A much wider problem was raised by the doctrine contained in the texts concerning colleges, guilds, companies, and other associations within the state. The Digest lays down elaborate rules concerning the rights and obligations of the parties in a *societas*, which is defined as a partnership of two or more persons "for their greater profit"; these rules would have immediate relevance for the development of the medieval law of trading partnerships.[15] On the other hand, under the title *Cuiuscumque universitatis* there is put forward an apparently very restrictive view of all kinds of association, beginning with a sweeping

[13] Constitution *Omnem* in proem to Digest.
[14] See below, p. 44.
[15] Digest 17. 2, *Pro socio*.

opinion of the jurist Gaius to the effect that *societates, collegia,* and the like are not allowed everywhere and for all, for these matters are restrained by the law and such bodies are conceded only for limited and specific reaons.[16] The examples given— partnerships of farmers of the public tolls, washers of gold and silver, exploiters of salt pans, and shipowners and bakers in Rome—are not very helpful, so that the comment of the medieval gloss is, not unexpectedly "since certain collegia are permitted, it is apparent that as a rule [*regulariter*] they are prohibited." The conflict with the *de facto* situation in the Italian cities must have seemed stark enough in Irnerius's day, but it had become much worse by the end of the twelfth century as all kinds of societies, colleges, guilds, and confraternities burgeoned in profusion in the free cities of Italy. Of course, texts could be found to justify certain types of association, such as religious fraternities, but what could be said of the noble tower societies, which were electing their own officials, exacting oaths from their members, and passing what they called *acta, statuta,* and *ordinamenta* which regulated, among other things, the descent of property for their members, a matter which should obviously have been regulated by the public law.[17] Then, in the thirteenth century, there appeared the *societates populi,* political associations of artisans and citizens of the middle rank, who in the end succeeded in taking over control of most of the communes. It may have been with these in mind that Odofredo argued that any *corpus* formed to secure justice (*causa iusticie*) was legitimate under the *ius gentium,* but this was obviously straining the letter of the law very severely.[18] The policy of trying to put down associations within the Italian cities adopted from time to time by medieval emperors and despots had strong support from Roman law.

The question of corporations leads naturally to the broader problem of the relationship between local municipal law and the

[16] Digest 3. 4.

[17] F. Niccolai, "I consorzi nobiliari ed il comune nell'alta e media Italia," *Rivista di storia del diritto italiano* 12 (1940): 116–47, 292–341, 397–477.

[18] Odofredo, in Digest 3.4. The Accursian gloss legitimizes the student universities in this way.

ius commune, the general law of the empire.[19] In the *Corpus* it was quite clear that the *ius commune* prevailed over municipal law and local *consuetudines*, though a suggestion could be found that a law might be abrogated by long disuse, which implied the tacit consent of the whole community. Here again, the contrast between the situation *de facto* and *de iure* became more and more blatant as the volume of communal legislation gathered weight in the later twelfth and the early thirteenth century and the role of the emperor in the internal affairs of the cities was seen to diminish. It is unlikely that the practical men who were chiefly responsible for the framing and application of communal statutes lost much sleep over this. The statutes of even a minor commune like Como state explicitly in 1281 that justice must first be done according to the city statutes and, where these are lacking, according to the usage and good customs of the city; only when these too are lacking should recourse be made to the *leges* and *iura* of the civil law.[20] The academic lawyers were slow to follow where the less learned *statutarii* had led, and in academic writings it was not generally admitted until the early fourteenth century that local statutes actually prevailed over the common law.

It is clear that the hard line taken by the academic lawyers with regard to local law and custom goes back to Irnerius, for in a gloss which is generally accepted as his he comments upon the text that laws might be abrogated by disuse implying common consent: "This law is speaking according to its own times. . . . today power has been transferred to the emperor."[21] The only obvious way in which this clash might be resolved was by an imperial confirmation of local *consuetudines*, such as that obtained by the citizens of Bologna from Emperor Henry V in 1116.[22]

---

[19] There is an excellent survey of this problem in Stelling-Michaud, *L'Université de Bologne*, pp. 55–59.

[20] The thirteenth-century statutes of Verona used similar wording; see P. S. Leicht, "La penetrazione del movimento bolognese nella vita giuridica dell'Emilia e dell'Italia settentrionale," *Studi*, n.s., 1 (1956):151, n. 2.

[21] H. Kantorowicz, *Studies in the Glossators of Roman Law* (Cambridge, 1938), pp. 135f.

[22] Edited and discussed by L. Simeoni, "Bologna e la politica italiana di Enrico V," *AMDSP* 2 (1937):147–66.

Similar grants to enjoy their ancient customs had been given to cities long before,[23] but the presence of Irnerius as a prominent witness to this diploma suggests that, in his mind at least, the theoretical significance of what the Emperor was conceding was appreciated. Two generations later, the glosses to the Peace of Constance of 1183 between Frederick Barbarossa and the Lombard League show the jurists interpreting the treaty as legitimizing the statutes of the cities named in the treaty.[24]

The imperial diploma of 1116 is also valuable for the light it throws on the internal government of Bologna at a crucial moment of its development. Here it is necessary to distinguish between the two parts of the document. The first comprises a highly formalized grant to the citizens of their ancient *consuetudines*, providing general protection of their rights and specific measures in favor of the Bolognese merchants, together with a significant provision releasing the citizens' tenants from any hospitality tax (*albergaria*) which might be levied by the count. In this section, the only hint of the existence of the commune is the clause which states that fines for infringement shall be divided equally between the imperial fisc and the citizens (*concivibus*). This may be compared with the corresponding clause in Henry IV's diploma to the citizens of Lucca in 1081, where the division was between the imperial camera and the injured party.[25] The change suggests that by 1116 the citizen-body had developed some kind of treasury into which such payments could be made. The second part of the privilege is much less formal and is concerned with the pardon granted by the Emperor for the destruction of the royal palace in Bologna, which had apparently taken place after the death of Countess Matilda the year before. The precise terms by which this pardon is extended—"as to the Bolognese *popolo* itself, so also to all who gave help"—suggests that the word *popolo* is being used

---

[23] E.g., to the inhabitants of Genoa in 958: see L. Schiaparelli, *I diplomi di Ugo e di Lotaro, di Berengario e di Adalberto*, FSI [Fonti per la Storia d'Italia] (Rome, 1924), pp. 326–27.

[24] Leicht, "La penetrazione del movimento bolognese," pp. 126–27.

[25] J. Ficker, *Urkunden zur Reichs- und Rechtsgeschichte Italiens* (Innsbruck, 1874), vol. 4, pp. 124–25.

not in a vague sense, to indicate the inhabitants in general, but to denote the specific members of a sworn association, the commune. This suspicion is strengthened by a document of 1123 in which the consuls of the Bolognese commune are mentioned for the first time: they make a promise on their own behalf and in the name of the bishop "with our whole Bolognese *popolo*," and specify that the agreement is to be ratified "by the said *popolo*, through the oath of obedience which it makes to us."[26] Here it is quite clear that *popolo* means the commune, which is bound to its officials, the consuls, by an oath which is periodically renewed. As for the leaders of the commune in 1116, although they are not given the title "consuls," it is tempting to identity them as the eight Bolognese named as present at the reception of the imperial diploma, together with Alberto Grasso and Ugo de Ansaldo, who are saddled with the responsibility for the original rising against the palace. Whatever its significance at the moment of its reception, there can be no doubt that the privilege of 1116 was seen in retrospect as the foundation charter of the Bolognese commune and, as such, was placed at the beginning of the great chartulary of the commune, known as the *Registro grosso*, compiled by the learned notary Raniero da Perugia in 1226.

If the Bolognese commune was already in existence in 1116, the question arises as to why it was not more clearly referred to, especially in the more formal part of the diploma. Here the unofficial, provisional, and even temporary character of the early communes must be remembered. The leaders of the commune may well have been chary of pushing it to the fore in a document which was intended to safeguard their rights for a long time to come. Again, the Emperor's advisers may have been doubtful about extending any kind of official recognition to a new and untried institution which could easily turn toward subversive acts; it was a long time before the communes found their way into the public law of the Empire. Finally, if Irnerius was asked his professional opinion, there is not much doubt that

[26] Registro grosso, fol. 12; Savioli, *Annali bolognesi*, vol. 1, no. 2, doc. 109.

he would have advised against any recognition of the commune, an entity unknown to the civil law and contrary to it in both letter and spirit. The first formal intervention of the law school in Bolognese affairs is likely to have been a negative one.

The attraction of the medieval Empire for Irnerius is proved by the fact that for several years after 1116 he became a follower of Henry V. According to a contemporary Milanese writer, he played a leading part in the creation in Rome in 1118 of the imperialist anti-pope, Gregory VIII, and he was the only layman excommunicated for his adhesion to the Anti-Pope by the Council of Rheims the following year.[27] In his imperialism, as in many other things, Irnerius established a tradition which remained strong in the Bolognese school for a long time. His pupils and successors, the famous Four Doctors, are celebrated for their association with Frederick Barbarossa and his attempt to resuscitate the imperial régime in Italy. This is not the place for a discussion of the decrees of Roncaglia, where the Emperor is supposed to have taken the advice of the jurists as to the extent of the imperial *regalia*, but it may be noted in passing that although the revival of Roman practice was relatively simple in technical matters like the drawing up of documents or court procedure, as soon as they entered the political sphere the jurists encountered the cross-currents of a totally alien way of thinking, and the result was generally a curious hybrid, neither truly Roman nor entirely medieval in character.

The unsatisfactory results likely to ensue from the meeting of academic lawyers and a barbarian emperor stand out clearly from an examination of the Authentic *Habita*, whose provisions in favor of "all those scholars who wander for the cause of study" and who "are made exiles for the love of knowledge, especially the professors of divine and holy laws," represent an attempt to bring the growing student world of Italy under direct imperial protection. Intended for insertion in the Code, the *Habita* was issued at Roncaglia in 1158 and appears to have

[27] De Vergottini, "Lo studio di Bologna, l'impero e il papato," *Studi*, n.s., 1 (1956): 30–33.

been a confirmation of a privilege granted to representatives of the Bolognese schools who had met Barbarossa near the city some three years before.[28] Its drafting seems to reveal the ideas of the Italian jurists blended with those of the Emperor's advisers. The outlook of the imperial chancellery is most apparent in the preamble and the provisions concerning freedom of travel and general protection; the Bolognese commentators of later generations, to whom these appeared superfluous in content and over-rhetorical in language, interpreted them as exempting scholars from the payment of tolls.[29]

The second section of the *Habita* dealt with the problem of scholars living outside their native city who might be held responsible for the debts of their fellow citizens, whether students, merchants, or others, by the authorities of the city in which they were studying. The Emperor exempted all students and teachers from such reprisals under pain of very severe penalties, not only against those who effected such confiscations but also against officials who failed to secure restitution. This provision was a response to the grievance which had apparently induced the doctors to seek the Emperor's help in the first place, and that it was regarded by them as the most important part of the Authentic is indicated by the direction that it should be placed in the Code under the title *Ne filius pro patre*, which dealt with the analogous case of a son held responsible for his father's debts. This was a very reasonable and useful addition to the law, provided, of course, that it could be enforced.

[28] The *Habita* is edited, with discussion, by H. Koeppler in *English Historical Review* 54 (1939):577–607. For more recent views, see Cencetti, "Studium fuit Bononie," p. 317f. I was unable to see the article by Marongiu, "Alle origini dell'università: la costituzione «Habita» di Federico Barbarossa," *Rivista guiridica della scuola* 5 (1966). In view of the speculations of several writers, it should be stressed that the sole evidence for the privilege of 1155 is the contemporary *Carmen de gestis Frederici I Imperatoris in Lombardia*, Scriptores Rerum Germanicarum (Hanover, 1965), pp. 16–17, and all suggestions as to how this may have differed from the *Habita* are purely conjecture.

[29] Odofredo, in Code 4. 14 (*Authentica Habita*); W. Ullmann, "The Medieval Interpretation of Frederick I's Authentic 'Habita,'" *Europa e il diritto romano, studi in memoria di P. Koschaker* (Milan, 1954), vol. 1, p. 111. Odofredo's lectures were published at Lyons in 1550–52 as follows: vols. 1–3, Code; vols. 4–8, Digest.

Almost at the end of the *Habita*, as if it were an afterthought, the Emperor passes to a completely different subject. The text grants to scholars who might find themselves the defendants in any kind of lawsuit the option of having their case heard either by their own *dominus* or *magister* or by the bishop of the city in which they are residing. This provision can be seen both as a regularization of an already existing custom and as an attempt to revive an ancient law which had fallen into disuse. The classical model for this measure was a section of the constitution *Omnem* which made the governor of the province, the bishop, and the professors of law responsible for controlling the boisterous games indulged in by the law students of sixth-century Berytus. It is highly unlikely that Justinian's legislators intended to convey here any kind of regular jurisdiction, but this is how the Bolognese jurists understood the constitution. Odofredo's comment, for example, is that professors of civil law are thereby made the ordinary judges of their scholars, together with the bishop and the provincial governor.[30] The *Habita* was therefore interpreted as granting professors a jurisdiction over their students, yet while they were trying to imitate Justinian, the jurists had arrived at a typically medieval arrangement analogous to the position of a master of a craft guild vis-à-vis his apprentices.

One matter concerning the *Habita* on which the sources are tantalizingly obscure is that of the degree of corporate organization which had been achieved by the Bolognese academic community at this time. The fact that the Bolognese doctors took the initiative in petitioning for this law strongly suggests that they had formed some kind of organized body, if only for this specific purpose. On the other hand, the Emperor's response, at least in the only form in which we have it, not only makes no reference to any such body but also avoids naming Bologna or, indeed, any other center of learning. The *Habita* is deliberately framed in the widest possible terms so as to apply to any student or master in any subject, wherever he might be so long as he was outside his own city. This was no doubt thought appropriate

[30] Odofredo, in Digest 1.1.

in a text which was to be incorporated in the universal law, but the question remains why the Bolognese jurists did not seize their opportunity and secure a specific privilege which would in their eyes have established their school on the firmest possible foundations. The problem may well have been not that there was no organization, but that there were too many and of the wrong kind. It seems, for example, that it was customary at this time for a master and his students to be regarded as kind of *societas*; doctors refer to their pupils as their *socii*, and about 1175 Pilleo da Medicina complained that he had been held on account of the debts of his *socii*.[31] Indeed, the *Habita* can be regarded as recognizing the existence of *societates* of this kind by formally consolidating the position of each doctor at the head of his own little company of pupils. At the other extreme, it is likely that there already existed the general assembly of the whole academic community, doctors and scholars, which was referred to as the *"communi audientia magistrorum atque scholarium"* in a letter of Pope Clement III in 1189–91. A story in Boncompagno da Signa's *Rhetorica antiqua*, published in 1215, shows that in his time the whole academic community might gather in the cathedral to hear a dispute between two rival teachers and their pupils.[32] Boncompagno's account makes this sound a very informal and tumultuous assembly, the academic equivalent of the civic *concio* or *parlamentum* which all the inhabitants of the city had the right to attend. It is unlikely that such a large and heterogenous body would have been regarded as fit to receive imperial recognition in 1155–58.

The crux of the matter is whether there was already in being at the time of the *Habita* a society of doctors such as is first reported by Boncompagno in the period 1200–1215, when its functions included the appointment of doctors and the hearing and approval of new books.[33] The problem is oddly analogous

---

[31] Pilleo da Medicina, *Summa in tres libros*, cited by F. C. von Savigny, *Geschichte des Römischen Rechts im Mittelalter* (Heidelburg, 1850), vol. 4, pp. 312–14.

[32] C. Sutter, *Aus Leben und Schriften des Magisters Boncompagno* (Freiburg and Leipzig, 1894), pp. 44–45.

[33] Rashdall, *Universities of Europe*, vol. 1, pp. 146, 232.

to that of the Bolognese commune in 1116: the general situation seems to require the existence of a body to which no specific reference can be found. Some of the reasons for this apparent paradox may have been the same in both cases. Just as the civil law discouraged the recognition of an irregular body like the commune, so it offered no obvious opening for the creation of a corporate body with academic functions. The hint contained in the constitution *Omnem*, where control of the student revels was entrusted to the professors of Berytus, presumably acting as a body, was not followed up in the *Habita*, which speaks only of the individual *dominus* or *magister*. The *societas* of the Roman law texts was directed toward profit and the administration of common funds and property, and at this stage it is highly unlikely that the Bolognese doctors had any common property interests which would have prompted them to assume the legal standing of a *corpus* or *societas*. A century after the *Habita* the case of a *societas* without *corporalia* was recognized as a special problem by Odofredo, who expressed the opinion that the doctors and scholars of his day were, strictly speaking, not *socii* but *contubernales*—mere bedfellows—on the grounds that they did not combine together for profit.[34] He tells a revealing story about two teachers of grammar, one of whom was popular and the other unpopular, who agreed to specialize in different aspects of the subject and pool their earnings. Odofredo did not say that this agreement was illegal, but he clearly felt it to be inappropriate, presumably on the ground that knowledge and academic talent could not properly constitute *corporalia*.[35]

There were, therefore, certain obstacles of a theoretical kind to the incorporation of a society of doctors according to a strict interpretation of the civil law, but one may hazard a guess that these could have been overcome if there had not been other drawbacks of a more practical nature. A privilege granted to the Bolognese doctors of law, however general in its phraseology, would have bound the law school irrevocably to Bologna. The wanderings of many of the doctors of this period prove that the

[34] Odofredo, in Digest 3.4.1.
[35] *Ibid.*, 17.2.

schools were still very much mobile institutions, and a doctor's ability to decamp with his *societas* of pupils was a far more effective guarantee of academic freedom than any kind of imperial recognition. The doctors valued their freedom—from one another as much as from outside interference; even such an obvious move as the imperial designation of Bologna as a *civitas regia* might have impaired the freedom of movement upon which their academic liberty depended. So the Bolognese professors of law of the mid-twelfth century failed to assert the idea of an academic community under their leadership and control. For all its solemn form, the Authentic *Habita* authorized a régime more appropriate to a cottage industry than to an institution of higher learning. The failure to devise any form of central control left the professors in a weak position not just in the face of political pressures but also vis-à-vis the student body.

*The Formation of the University
and the Bolognese Commune*

It was the growing power of the Bolognese commune which was the first to take advantage of the weakness of the professorial organization. In common with the other major cities of northern Italy, Bologna advanced considerably along the road to practical self-government during the second half of the twelfth century, especially during the conflict with Barbarossa. A rebellion against the imperial *podestà* in 1161 was rapidly put down by Frederick in person, but in December 1167 Bologna joined the Lombard League against the Emperor, and until the Truce of Venice in 1177 the law school, with its imperialist traditions, must have passed through a difficult period in the city. When peace was restored, the commune emerged greatly strengthened and with its sense of corporate identity much more strongly felt than before. It was during the struggle that two visible symbols of the unity of the commune, the single supreme official, called the *podestà*, and the decorated ox cart bearing the insignia of the city in battle, called the *carroccio*, made their appearance in Bologna. Both of them, it may be noted in passing, were movable, and they anticipated by a generation or so the first public buildings expressly built for the commune.[36] The commune had grown used to mobilizing its resources for war; now, in peace, the restored law school was clearly too great an asset to the economy of the city to escape the attention of the government for long. According to Pilleo da Medicina, it was in 1182 that the communal authorities tried to forestall a migration of doctors from the city by exacting an oath from them that they would not teach elsewhere for two years.[37] This measure was not entirely effective and was certainly contrary to the spirit of the *Habita*. However, the commune persisted, and in 1189 the jurist Lothario of Cremona was required to take a similar oath.[38] Thirty-seven years later this oath was considered sufficiently important to be included in the *Registro grosso*, in whose pages Lothario appears in distinguished company among the counts and nobles, clans, castles, and minor communes which had been compelled over the years to make their submission to the Bolognese commune. Moreover, it is clear from the text that Lothario did not submit without argument, for he extracted from the consuls the promise that the commune would neither compel him to teach nor prohibit him from teaching in the future in Bologna. However, even this most honorable capitulation was still a surrender of an essential element in the freedom of the law school, and thereafter the oath became customary for foreign doctors who wished to teach in Bologna. This encroachment by the commune could only have been resisted by a strong college of doctors in which those who were Bolognese citizens might have made common cause with the foreigners in the interest of academic freedom. As this structure was lacking, a vital part of the régime implicit in the *Habita* was swept away.

In the last decade of the twelfth century, while the doctors were losing ground before the commune, and possibly in reaction against this development, the universities of foreign students

[36] *Corpus chronicorum Bononiensium*, ed. A. Sorbelli, RIS 18 (Bologna, 1910–40), vol. 2, pp. 37, 43.
[37] Savigny, *Geschichte des Romischen Rechts*, vol. 4, pp. 312–14.
[38] *Chartularium studii Bononiensis* (Bologna, 1909), vol. 1, pp. 3–4.

were taking shape.[39] The later structure of the universities suggests that they were formed by the federation of a number of pre-existing student guilds with the usual religious, charitable, and social functions, whose membership was based on country or region of origin. At an unknown date, but certainly some time before 1204, these bodies had grouped themselves into four universities (later two), probably at the same time electing representative officials called rectors. This step, which was of such enormous importance for the future of the academic world, took place against a background of similar developments among the trading and artisan classes of the city. An unsupported chronicle statement that the seven consuls in office in 1174 were elected by the *societates* has been regarded with skepticism by most historians, but in 1194 Guido da Terrafogli, "*rector societatum*," appears with Calanchino, "*consul mercatorum*," as a witness to a commercial agreement between the communes of Bologna and Ferrara.[40] This suggests that by that date there existed some form of association linking the guilds of merchants, moneylenders, and moneychangers, a class whose growing importance is indicated by the imperial grant of a mint to the city three years before.[41] The organization of a union within this comparatively compact class may well have stimulated the students to attempt their own much larger and more complex association. The universities, in their turn, could have provided a model to be copied by the Bolognese artisan class, which, by 1219 at least, was beginning to make its influence felt in the political life of the city. In November 1228, the Bolognese artisans created their own union, which adopted the old name of *popolo* and rose in arms against the existing régime.[42] Over the next half century the Bolognese *popolo* developed a structure extraordinarily com-

---

[39] Rashdall, *Universities of Europe*, vol. 1, pp. 148f.; Rossi, "«Universitas scholarium» e comune," pp. 186–89.

[40] Registro grosso, fol. 60v; Savioli, *Annali bolognesi*, vol. 2, pt. 2, n. 302.

[41] Savioli, *Annali bolognesi*, vol. 2, no. 2, n. 298.

[42] Hessel, *Geschichte der Stadt Bologna*, pp. 332f. The documents relating to the Bolognese *popolo* were published by A. Gaudenzi, *Statuti delle società del popolo di Bologna*, FSI, 2 vols. (Rome, 1889–96); they are discussed by G. Fasoli in "Le compagnie delle armi a Bologna" and "Le compagnie delle arti a Bologna," *L'Archiginnasio* 28 (1933) and 30–31 (1935–36).

plex even by the high standards set by medieval Italian institutions, with a dual organization of trade-based guilds (*società d'arti*) and territorially based military companies (*società d'armi*) which make the universities with their constituent *nationes* and *conciliarie* appear almost models of simplicity. Given their very different membership and functions, detailed resemblances between the universities and the *popolo* are hardly to be looked for; however, one important characteristic which they seem to have shared is that of being based on an oath which was periodically renewed. In the case of the *popolo* it is certain that the constituent oath was renewed by the members in November 1233, exactly five years after its original formation; with regard to the universities, the settlement of a conflict which arose with the commune over the rectors' oath can best be explained if it is assumed that this too was subject to revision after a fixed term of years.[43] If this is true, it would underline the point that the universities and the *popolo* were institutions of a similar kind, both arising out of the common matrix of ideas and customs in Bolognese and north Italian society around the end of the twelfth century.

The creation of the student universities was bound to affect relations with the doctors, and it in fact revolutionized them very rapidly. There could be no objection to the student bodies in their function as charitable and welfare associations, and indeed there is no reason to doubt that some professors became members of the universities and this practice continued until at least the early fourteenth century.[44] But with the creation of the rectorate, which claimed to regulate the whole student body and challenged the jurisdiction of the doctors, conflict was inevitable. The jurists objected that the students, being only apprentices who were not yet qualified to practice their profession, were precluded by the civil law from electing consuls or rectors, just as were the apprentices of the skinners or any other

[43] See below, p. 43.

[44] A. Gaudenzi, "Appunti per servire alla storia dell'università di Bologna e dei suoi maestri," *L'Università* 3 (1889):158–211; for an example in 1308, see Rashdall, *Universities of Europe*, vol. 1, p. 158, n. 3.

trade guild.[45] The comparison with artisans is revealing, but this academic argument ignored the point, very important in fact if not in law, that while the skinners' apprentices were dependent on their masters for their livelihood, in the university the situation was the other way round. Once the students had developed the power of collective action, they were not slow to impose conditions on their teachers. In the *Rhetorica antiqua*, Boncompagno gives a glimpse of some of the methods, such as boycotts of lectures and the withholding of fees, by which the students asserted their power.

By the time of the first extant university statutes in the early fourteenth century, the professional life of the law teachers was hemmed in by the most minute regulations enforced by the officials of the student universities, which seem to reduce the doctors to such a state of servitude as to be scarcely compatible with the dignity of their profession.[46] In medieval Italy, however, it seems that submission to detailed professional regulations was not considered degrading or incompatible with a considerable degree of authority and respect. The chief officials of the communes, the *podestà* and *capitani del popolo* and their judges, were closely bound by elaborate statutes which commonly went so far as to prohibit them from going out to dinner with private citizens; after their term of office was over, their actions were scrutinized by a committee of citizens and fines were levied for any infringement of the statutes.[47] Yet these officials were well rewarded and were sometimes commemorated in inscriptions and sculptures, and many of them, despite the letter of the law, succeeded in exerting great personal influence for good or ill. The same is true of the most eminent professors, who were often men of great prominence in public life whose advice was sought by communes and princes. Writing soon after 1200, Boncompagno relates how the young Bolognese teacher Ugolino Gosia was invited to become *podestà* of Ancona. "If the governor-

---

[45] Azzo, in Code 3.13.7 (Paris edition of 1581, p. 189), followed by Accursio and Odofredo, etc.

[46] Rashdall, *Universities of Europe*, vol. 1, pp. 195–97.

[47] V. Franchini, *Saggio di ricerche sull'istituto del podestà nei comuni medioevali* (Bologna, 1912), gives a good all-round picture of the office.

ship of this city is given to me at this time," Boncompagno has Ugolino say, "I would not dare to accept it without the permission of my students [*socii*], to whom I teach the laws and to whom I am held, and am both in authority and subservience [*quibus teneor, presum et subsum*]."[48]

These words were obviously carefully chosen—authority and subservience, *presum et subsum*—and there is no warrant for stressing the one more than the other. When Ugolino Gosia transferred from the schools of Bologna to the office of *podestà* in Ancona, he was passing from one form of distinguished service to another, and his example was followed by many doctors of law in the centuries that followed. The treatment of professors and communal officials indicates an attitude toward authority in Italy which was far from simple. In northern Europe the authority of a ruler was felt to be bound up with his prerogative to act freely in a wide range of circumstances, but in the Italian communes and universities the actions of those in authority were limited as closely as possible out of distrust of the individual, while the offices themselves continued to inspire considerable respect.

The student universities do not seem to have aroused any immediate opposition on the part of the Bolognese commune, a fact which may be related to the influence of the merchants and moneylenders over the commune in the 1190s, for they would be likely to have had many business contacts with the student community. However, in the first years of the thirteenth century, trouble broke out which led to a migration of students to Vicenza in 1204; in 1215, following a riot between Lombard and Tuscan students, a group of the latter with their professors seceded to Arezzo.[49] The commune countered these moves by increasingly stringent laws prohibiting doctors or citizens from counselling or in any way aiding or abetting such migrations— even the university booksellers were made to swear not to supply

---

[48] *Liber de obsidione Ancone*, ed. G. C. Zimolo, RIS 7, no. 3 (1937), pp. 153–55.

[49] Rashdall, *Universities of Europe*, vol. 1, p. 168; Rossi, "«Universitas scholarium» e comune," pp. 219–25.

books to students living outside the city. In 1217 and 1220, the commune took the logical step of extending the oath against leaving Bologna to the student rectors. The rectors took the view that this demand was incompatible with the oath to maintain academic freedom to which they had been bound by the universities on taking office; to save them from perjury, the universities went to the length of abolishing the rectorate. The students appealed to the Pope, who took their side all the more readily as he was already at loggerheads with the commune over some of the lands of the Matildine inheritance. A papal letter of 1224 shows that the conflict had recently broken out again, for the rectors had ordered the migration of the whole academic body. This decision had been defied by the doctors, whom the Pope accused of being more concerned with private gain than with the public good.[50] The conclusion of this struggle is obscure, but it seems likely that advantage was taken of a renewal of the rectors' oath to insert some face-saving formula. The communal statutes of the second half of the thirteenth century show that the city government was successful in exacting the oath, though it did not entirely prevent further secessions of students.[51]

From the point of view of the future, the most important development of these years was the founding of rival universities at Padua in about 1220 and Naples in 1224.[52] The imperial foundation of Naples does not seem to have constituted a serious counterattraction for students, except for those from Frederick II's territories, but, together with his politically inspired ban on the Bolognese schools, it did represent a serious ideological threat, while the migration to Padua, which was far more successful than the earlier student migrations, showed that the wandering tradition was still alive and potentially dangerous. It would seem to be in reaction to these events that we find the jurist Azzo teaching that the legend of San Petronio, a piece of pseudo-

[50] Savioli, *Annali bolognesi*, vol. 2, no. 2, pp. 56–57.
[51] G. Fasoli and P. Sella, *Statuti di Bologna dell'anno 1288* (Rome, 1937), vol. 1, pp. 95–96.
[52] Rashdall, *Universities of Europe*, vol. 2, pp. 10–14, 22–24.

history written in the 1170s telling how Bologna had been rebuilt by Emperor Theodosius at the request of St. Ambrose, was tantamount to the designation of Bologna as a *civitas regia*.[53] Azzo's interpretation of this supposed privilege was so territorial in spirit that he even argued that the schools held in his day at San Stefano were illegal because they were outside the boundaries of the ancient city, to which the imperial privilege alone applied. About the same time, the missing Theodosian privilege was "forged" by someone who was probably a student of rhetoric—it was embellished by such bizzare details that it is possible that it was intended as a joke.[54] Nevertheless, it found its way into the communal chancellery and, after some hesitation, was added to the *Registro grosso* in the 1270s. While Azzo's views represented a final break with the idea of the mobile *societates* of the twelfth century, the Theodosian legend could be accepted without reserve by the civic authorities because it operated entirely to the advantage of the city.

Whether it was because the Bolognese monopoly was now definitely broken or because of a change in the political atmosphere following the ascendency of the Bolognese *popolo* after 1228, the 1230s opened a new chapter in the relations between the academic community and the commune.[55] In return for promises not to desert the city, the students received a series of privileges and various forms of special protection which were summed up in the doctrine that they enjoyed the advantage of citizen status but not its disadvantages and that they were the special sons of the *popolo*. The doctors were not so favored, for although they were exempted from military service, the policy of paying their salaries, which had been adopted in the 1220s, was dropped and only reintroduced in the 1280s.[56] The causes

[53] In Const. *Omnem*, cit. Odofredo. The Accursian gloss has "Ut referri dicunt in legenda b. Petronii"; those consulting the *Legenda*, ed. F. Lanzoni, (Rome, 1907), pp. 219–50, will find that it says nothing of the kind.

[54] G. Fasoli and G. B. Pighi, "Il privilegio teodosiano," *Studi*, n.s. 2 (1961): 55–94.

[55] Though the extant statutes are later, Rossi ("«Universitas scholarium» e comune," pp. 219–25) argues that this was the decisive decade.

[56] *Ibid.*, p. 239.

of complaint among the students ceased to be so much direct aggression by the citizens as incidental injuries arising out of the bitter party conflicts which divided the city.

The most interesting aspect of the mid-thirteenth-century alliance between students and citizens is the way in which the privileges of the universities of foreign students (as they should, strictly speaking, be called, for Bolognese citizens were ineligible for membership) were assimilated to those of the *popolo*. For example, the academic community was placed under the special care of the *podestà* and the *capitano*, and the rectors were allowed immediate access to the highest officials of the commune, who were bound to summon the councils to hear their complaints if requested, a privilege otherwise restricted to the college of *anziani* and the heads of the guilds in their capacity as the leaders of the *popolo*.[57] Most significant of all, in 1274, a statute was passed allowing a student who was the victim of a violent crime to prove his accusation by obtaining the supporting oath of a university rector and a councilor of his "nation"; once this proof was presented to him, the *podestà* had no option but to take immediate action against the accused.[58] This law was clearly modeled on the anti-magnatial legislation of the time, which granted a similar procedure to a member of the *popolo* in cases of injury by a magnate. In a measure passed at the request of the rectors in 1274, the equivalence of the university and the *popolo* is explicitly stated in the words, "the university of scholars shall enjoy the privilege of the *other* societies of the *popolo* of Bologna in the buying of corn and other commodities from the commune."[59] It is in these laws that the universities and the association of the *popolo*, born through a similar process within a generation of each other, come closest together.

The purpose of this survey has been to suggest that the relations between political and academic institutions in Bologna in the twelfth and thirteenth centuries were much broader and

[57] *Statuti*, 1288, 1.97–98.
[58] A. Gaudenzi, "Lo studio di Bologna nei primi due secoli della sua esistenza," *Annuario dell'Università di Bologna* (1900–1901), pp. 170–71.
[59] *Statuti*, 1288, 1.100.

deeper than the story of their occasional clashes would lead one to suppose. Like the early communes, the universities were personal and not territorial, and they were mobile not only in theory but in practice. As a union of guilds, they resembled the *popolo*, many of whose special privileges they came to enjoy. The formative influence was not the doctrines of the civil law, which they violated in important respects, but the customs and pragmatic arrangements which arose in the life of the Italian cities as they developed virtually free from external control. The medieval Italian universities were typical products of their place and time, and their statutes express a particular attitude toward authority which belongs specifically to the age of the communes. It is amazing that, rooted as they were in the environment of the medieval city-state, the universities of the Italian type later showed such powers of adaptation to other social and political systems that, in a sense, they are still with us.

JACQUES VERGER

2 | The University of Paris at the End of the Hundred Years' War

Political society in its modern form appeared, as everybody knows, in Europe at the close of the Middle Ages. In France this decisive mutation was precipitated by the Hundred Years' War. Initially a feudal conflict, it became a national war because of its operational scale and its repercussions through every walk of life and every class of society. It was in such circumstances that the modern state affirmed its prerogatives and developed its power, while among the people a national consciousness was born and patriotism, in the fairly simple form exemplified in Joan of Arc, became a permanent feature of the French political makeup.

Politics then could no longer be the concern only of kings or the great barons; from that time on every social group had its own position on public affairs, and a body of public opinion took shape which the rulers of the land could not afford to ignore. This would explain, for instance, how the long and severe conflict between Orléanists and Burgundians, though it had originated in a quarrel between princes of the blood, in fact divided the whole of French society into two camps. In the very first rank of the groups which were called upon to adopt certain political attitudes toward current events, and to play a certain role in them, we find the University of Paris.

Certainly one cannot talk about this as an entirely new situation. Ever since their inception, all medieval universities

47

had been in one way or another confronted with the fact of .
politics. As autonomous institutions, they had to react to events,
to adapt themselves to changes in the political situation—in
short, to insert themselves as best they could, in both theory and
practice, into a given political society—be it kingdom, seigniory,
or commune, and to define their relations with other groups
in that society as well as with the holders of authority. In the
preceding chapter, for example, we saw what constituted the
relations between the university at Bologna and the imperial
and communal powers in the city during the twelfth and thirteenth centuries.

But at Paris in the fifteenth century this ancient problem was
posed in completely new terms. The differences between the
situation of the university at Bologna in the twelfth and thirteenth centuries and that which we shall examine here were
very considerable. First of all, the political organizations which
confronted the two universities were not identical. At Bologna
in the twelfth century the imperial power was remote and weak,
and as for the commune, it did not have very much authority at
its disposal. Itself founded on the principle of the sworn association, originally private and individual and then invested with
public power, the commune found nothing to object to in the
same structure of the university and in the development and
exercises of its privileges and autonomy. In fifteenth-century
France, on the other hand, this personal and contractual conception of political power no longer had relevance, and the
University of Paris found itself face to face with a state already
modern, national, and territorial. This state was a divine right
monarchy in which the slow work of the lawyers since the thirteenth century had resuscitated the Roman notions of absolute
authority concentrated in the person of the sovereign and of
common law, defined by the prince and applicable to all free
men throughout the entire realm.[1] In such a situation a corpora-

---

[1] Cf. B. Guenée, "L'Histoire de l'état en France à la fin du Moyen-Age
vue par les historiens français depuis cent ans," *Revue historique* 232 (1964):
331–60; B. Guenée, "Etat et nation en France au Moyen-Age," *Revue historique* 237 (1967):17–30.

tion as jealous of its ancient autonomy as the University of Paris necessarily found itself out of balance, and a readjustment was inevitable. This necessity weighed very heavily on the entire history we shall examine.

Moreover—and this second difference reinforces the effects of the first—the dominant intellectual preoccupations were not the same in the two universities. Bologna was consecrated above all to the study and glossing of Roman law. Doubtless this body of law could not be applied to medieval political realities, and adaptations and compromises were constantly required. But at least the Bolognese university community was prepared by these very studies to envisage political problems very realistically, that is to say, in fact, politically. It was aware that, within the sphere of human activity, politics constituted an autonomous, secular domain which was ruled by its own principles which, for the most part, had been established by Roman law. At Paris, on the other hand, civil law had been banished from the university since the thirteenth century. The university was dominated by the doctors of theology and, along with them, the canonists—all clerics. Accustomed to envisage all things from the points of view of theology and at the level of all Christendom, these academics were scarcely prepared for strict political analysis, and when faced with events their conceptions and attitudes were very different from those of Bologna.

This study will center on the period from 1418, when the Burgundians recaptured Paris, to 1450, when Charles VII successfully re-established his authority in the ancient Burgundian provinces and the war came to an end. I have chosen this period because it represents a culminating phase in the Hundred Years' War.[2] For the historian, political problems begin to replace military problems and move to the foreground. With the recapture of Paris by John the Fearless, the Armagnac and Burgundian break had become complete, and public opinion in

[2] For a general history of the war, see E. Perroy, *La Guerre de cent ans* (Paris, 1945); and for the period immediately before 1418, in particular, see A. Coville, *Jean Petit. La question du tyrannicide au commencement du XVe siècle* (Paris, 1932); A. Coville, *Les Cabochiens et l'ordonnance de 1413* (Paris, 1888).

France was henceforth divided into two violently antagonistic parties. Two years later the Treaty of Troyes, which was intended to re-establish peace, above all reinforced this split by setting up a precise political system for or against which the adversaries began fighting one another. Eliminating the last ambiguities of Burgundian politics, this treaty made the king of England, Henry V, the regent of the kingdom of France and the legitimate heir of the king of France, Charles VI. The two kingdoms of England and France, distinct but united in the person of the sovereign, would from now on be associated in a system of "double monarchy." The Duke of Burgundy, constituting in himself an autonomous principality in the Flemish and Burgundian domains, would be the guarantor of the system.

Such a personal union of two kingdoms was not without precedent in the Middle Ages, but at this time and in these circumstances it was a particularly ambitious and risky attempt. Around the Dauphin, Charles, a refugee in Bourges who had been disowned and disinherited by his relatives at Troyes, regrouped the Armagnac party and all those who rejected the double monarchy on the basis of patriotism—that is to say, on the basis of fidelity to the legitimate dynasty of the Valois and, above all, of hostility to the English, to whom the Treaty of Troyes threatened to give all important positions in the realm of France. In 1420 such a decision as that of the Treaty of Troyes could not be imposed without discussion, by a simple accord between sovereigns. All French public opinion reacted because a long history of war and political confrontations had given the country a certain national conscience and a certain sense of the state—a sense of the nature of the sovereign's authority and of its limits. In order to impose or resist the system created at Troyes, the English and French sovereigns needed help from the principal groups constituting French society at the time. The University of Paris, whose intellectual prestige and social role had been universally accepted for a long time, constituted one such group. It had been forced by the general political mentality of the age in the years 1420–50, as well as by events, to play a political role and to confront the great problems which were weighing on the contemporary conscience.

This subject will be dealt with in three sections. First, the political role played by the University of Paris, the nature of its interventions and their actual results, will be briefly recalled. We shall then try to discover the political goals of the university and the guidelines for its actions. Finally, we shall venture an interpretation of these facts. Why did the university adopt those attitudes and pursue those aims? What is revealed about its internal structure, its material and social condition, and the collective mentality of its members and their general conceptions of society and politics?

Let me make clear the intention and the method of this research. It is not concerned with the history of ideas or of political theories; rather, it is a practical investigation of behavior, a study in social and political psychology. Starting from the political acts of the university men, we shall try to trace the conceptions, the psychological realities (whether conscious or not) which might explain them. This is an attempt not to define their political theories but rather to understand in concrete terms the place of the University of Paris in the political life of fifteenth-century France. Diplomatic and narrative sources have been relied on, for the most part: the *Chartularium* of the university,[3] the chronicles of Paris,[4] the minutes of Joan of Arc's trial,[5] and the legal proceedings conducted by the university before the Parlement of Paris.[6]

It is with the Schism, in the latter part of the fourteenth century, that the notion of an official role for the University of

---

[3] H. Denifle and E. Chatelain, eds., *Chartularium Universitatis Parisiensis*, vol. 4: *(1394–1452)* (Paris, 1897), to which one must add H. Denifle and E. Chatelain, eds., *Auctarium chartularii Universitatis Parisiensis*, vol. 2: *Liber procuratorum nationis Anglicanae (Alemanniae) ab anno MCCCCVI usque ad annum MCCCCLXVI* (Paris, 1897); see also an older book, C.-E. du Boulay, *Historia Universitatis Parisiensis*, vol. 5: *(Ab anno 1400 ad annum 1500)* (Paris, 1670).

[4] A. Tuetey, ed., *Journal d'un bourgeois de Paris (1405–1449)* (Paris, 1881).

[5] J. Quicherat, ed., *Procès de condamnation et de réhabilitation de Jeanne d'Arc*, 5 vols. (Paris, 1841–49).

[6] Extracts of the Registres du Conseil can be found in A. Tuetey, ed., *Journal de Clément de Fauquembergue, greffier du Parlement de Paris (1417–1435)*, 3 vols. (Paris, 1903–15). We have also consulted the Registres des Plaidoiries at the Archives Nationales, vol. 1: *Matinées*, X1A 4794–X1A 4804; vol. 2: *Après-diners*, X1A 8302–X1A 8305.

Paris was born. The research of Noël Valois has revealed the part played by the university in that crisis and how it contributed to the outcome by its advice to the King of France and its dynamic action in the Councils.[7] The university men realized on that occasion that their vocation was not limited to teaching and intellectual pursuits within their autonomous corporation, that they might exert an influence upon the course of events, supply advice, and bestow their approval or censure. In this new vocation they very soon addressed themselves to national political issues, at a time when unrest was becoming widespread with the madness of Charles VI and the struggle between Orléanists and Burgundians. (One remembers the part played by the public controversy between Jean Petit and Gerson or the influence of the university during the period of Cabochian trouble.)

Let us begin with the year 1418. The university was not spared in the massacres following the capture of Paris by the Burgundians on 29 May.[8] Some ten regents and a number of students were killed; the College of Navarre was ransacked; many people, especially foreigners, departed, and others who happened to be away, such as Gerson, did not return. The university, if somewhat disabled after June, was unanimous in rallying to the support of the policies of John the Fearless. As early as August it issued a long proclamation summing up for the general public the charges laid by the Burgundians against the Orléanists.[9] In the following months the university adopted the policies of the Duke of Burgundy even in their inconsistencies —for instance, after presenting the defense of Rouen as an issue of national solidarity, it reconciled itself to the surrender of that city without any qualms;[10] again, after encouraging the project of negotiation with the Dauphin, it gave that up after the assassination of John the Fearless at Montereau.[11] These shifts

---

[7] N. Valois, *La France et le grand schisme d'Occident*, 4 vols. (Paris, 1896–1901).

[8] L. Bellaguet, ed., *Chronique du religieux de Saint-Denis, contenant le règne de Charles VI, de 1380 à 1422*, vol. 6 (Paris, 1852), bk. 39, pp. 234–35; Denifle and Chatelain, eds., *Auctarium*, vol. 2, cols. 246–47.

[9] Denifle and Chatelain, eds., *Chartularium*, vol. 4, no. 2107.

[10] *Ibid.*, nos. 2120, 2125.

[11] Tuetey, ed., *Clément de Fauquembergue*, 1: 269–70, 331–33; Denifle and Chatelain, eds., *Chartularium*, vol. 4, nos. 2144, 2149.

indicate above all that the university no longer had a determining influence within the Burgundian party, and it did not pretend to draw up a political program. For the most part, it was an institution on whose prestige the Duke of Burgundy would draw when he wished to issue a solemn declaration to impress public opinion (or, at any rate, that of Paris), and such acts did not allow the university any degree of initiative to attempt to alter the course of events or impose views of its own.

Furthermore, the university did not act independently but with other groups of Parisian leaders whose collaboration the government secured in order to reinforce its own authority, such as members of Parlement, the Paris clergy, the provost of the merchants, the aldermen, etc. Members of the university can be found, for instance, in the assemblies frequently summoned by the Duke between 1418 and 1420 to administer the city of Paris, especially in his absence.[12] They can also be found among the councilors of Philip the Good at Troyes, men such as Pierre Cauchon or Jean Beaupère.[13]

After 1420 Paris was placed under the double monarchy system. Power was in the hands of the English regents, Henry V and, after him, the Duke of Bedford, but, at some distance, Philip the Good remained a powerful protector, indeed, the mainstay of the régime.[14] The university adopted the double monarchy at once and twice pledged itself to observe the Treaty of Troyes, first through its representatives on 30 May, then individually on 4 and 5 June,[15] the latter occasion probably a very spectacular one. This collaboration was maintained during the next few years: here its principal episodes and general character will simply be reviewed.[16]

On every suitable occasion, the university would issue proclamations, sing masses, or walk in procession to celebrate the

---

[12] Tuetey, ed., *Clément de Fauquembergue*, vol. 1, passim.
[13] Denifle and Chatelain, eds., *Chartularium*, vol. 4, no. 2155.
[14] Cf. C. A. J. Armstrong, "La double monarchie France-Angleterre et la maison de Bourgogne (1420–1435). Le déclin d'une alliance," *Annales de Bourgogne* 37 (1965):81–112.
[15] Denifle and Chatelian, eds., *Chartularium*, vol. 4, nos. 2160–61.
[16] One can find a brief survey in C. Jourdain, "L'Université de Paris à l'époque de la domination anglaise," *Excursions historiques et philosophiques à travers le Moyen-Age* (Paris, 1888), pp. 309–35.

victories of the Anglo-Burgundians which announced a definitive restoration of peace, and the people of Paris were invited to share in these public rejoicings. When a dispute between the Duke of Gloucester and Philip the Good in 1424 seemed to threaten the very basis of the double monarchy system, the university was prompt to act as moderator.[17] There is no need to dwell on the single most important event of those years, Joan of Arc's trial. The university, admittedly, was not in charge, yet its contribution to the special bias of the prosecution and to the sentence itself was considerable. It had asked that Joan be tried by a religious tribunal as soon as she was taken prisoner; it sent some of its more illustrious members, such as Jean Beaupère and Thomas de Courcelles, to cross-examine her with Bishop Cauchon; and it called upon its faculties to assemble and investigate the charges against her. Six months later, it was the representative of the university, Nicolas Midi, who greeted the young Henry VI as he entered Paris on the way to Notre-Dame for his coronation. His speech, the draft of which has been preserved in the *Chartularium*, declares without the least ambiguity the support of the university for the double monarchy:

The university, its rector, its faculties, its nations, and all its members are at the disposal of our sovereign lord to serve him, each according to his proper vocation. The university renders thanks to God for the joyous and happy accession of the King, prays for his safety and the success of his enterprises, and, through the whole kingdom, will organize prayers, speeches, processions, and sermons exhorting the people to join in our good wishes.[18]

There is another aspect that should not be overlooked. The main object here is to study the university as a collective entity, yet we should not forget that many of those who had been its

[17] Denifle and Chatelain, eds., *Chartularium*, vol. 4, nos. 2248–49.

[18] "Universitas offert se ipsam, suum rectorem, singulas facultates, nationes et supposita ad beneplacita et obsequia domini nostri regis secundum suam professionem. . . . Dicta Universitas offert pro referendo gratias Deo de jocundo et prospero adventu domini nostri regis predicti et deprecando pro incolumitate ejus felicique suorum agendorum successu ac tocius regni preces, orationes, processiones et predicationes ad populum, ut similiter deprecetur, exhortatorias" (*ibid.*, no. 2399).

members advanced to brilliant careers in the higher ranks of the clergy or the households of princes. Pierre Cauchon is, of course, a case in point, but there were a great many others. In the north of France quite a few of these men became important figures in the Anglo-Burgundian party, and they often sought the recommendation of the university in order to obtain a place or a benefice.[19] As a rule, the university, out of professional solidarity rather than political conviction, did not object, so that, without always meaning to, the university appeared to the people as all the more committed to the Anglo-Burgundian party. On the other hand, the latter was sometimes granted special favors— for instance, degrees were conferred upon some of its members even when they had not served the prescribed period of time as students.[20]

From 1420 to 1435, then, the university continued to side with the Anglo-Burgundians, but it is the specific character and the limitation of this collaboration which ought to be stressed. First of all, within that party the university belonged to the moderate wing. Apart from their fanatical attitude about Joan of Arc (a fanaticism more religious than political), it may be said that the doctors were usually cautious and inclined toward pacifism—their ambassadors, for instance, assisted Philip the Good in 1432 in his first attempt at negotiating with Charles VII.[21] But, above all, what has been said above concerning an earlier period (1418–20) still held true: the university no longer had any determining role, it did not draft any political program, and it took no initiative. Its interventions were, in fact, solicited by the authorities themselves, who wished to further their own ends with the help of this much respected advocate. Its activities were mostly ceremonial: speeches, sermons, processions, banquets, masses, etc. By those means the university could exert a a real influence, and it is likely that the Sunday sermons in particular fostered a lasting hostility to Charles VII among the people of Paris—the *Journal d'un bourgeois de Paris* is very telling

---

[19] *Ibid.*, nos. 2163 or 2167; Tuetey, ed., *Clément de Fauquembergue*, 2:24.
[20] Denifle and Chatelain, eds., *Chartularium*, vol. 4, nos. 2303, 2310.
[21] *Ibid.*, no. 2420.

in this respect[22]—but this was a role of minor importance. The university had no influence upon the great decisions of state, it held no commanding position, and often it was merely associated with other groups of notables. Even at the trial of Joan of Arc, the Parisian doctors merely acted as attendants upon Cauchon and the canons of Rouen.

Actually, the essential problem for the university and the ordinary occasion of its contact with the authorities was the defense of its own material interests, principally the confirmation and observance of its privileges. Officially, the Anglo-Burgundian government showed a benevolent interest in the university: its privileges were several times confirmed between 1418 and 1422 by Charles VI and Henry V.[23] In practice, however, several occasions of conflict persisted, although both parties were of course agreed not to let them break out into the open. Yet the requests from the university and the legal proceedings before the Parlement are sufficient proof that the royal agents kept violating the university franchises, by levying taxes on the students and prosecuting them before public tribunals.[24]

[22] It is known that the author of this anonymous chronicle, although most certainly a cleric and member of the university, reflects above all the opinion of the average Parisian bourgeois. Always ready to distrust the English, he had esteem only for the Duke of Burgundy. On the other hand, up to 1436 and beyond, he detested Charles VII and his partisans and never stopped enumerating the crimes of these "Armagnacs," as he continually called them. According to him, the Peace of Arras was only a trick against the Parisians ("en celui conseil ne firent rien qui proufitast à Paris"). After 1436 the Parisian bourgeois did not deny the legitimacy of Charles VII, but for him this sovereign seemed even more remote and indifferent to the interests of Parisians than the English sovereign ("le roy se despartit de Paris le troisiesme jour de décembre mil quatre cents trente sept, sans ce que nul bien y feist à la ville de Paris pour lors; et sembloit qu'il ne fust venu seulement que pour veoir la ville"). Manifestly, the Parisian bourgeois is completely immune to the patriotic values of which Charles VII was the incarnation for most Frenchmen.

[23] Tuetey, ed., Clément de Fauquembergue, vol. 1, p. 226; Denifle and Chatelain, eds., Chartularium, vol. 4, nos. 2165, 2178, 2214.

[24] For instance, in 1427 the university interceded to rescue Bernard Nivart, a doctor of medicine, and Robin le Tardif, a student of canon law, imprisoned by order of the Parlement (Matinées, X1A 4795, fol. 113v–114, for B. Nivart; Tuetey, ed., Clément de Fauquembergue, 2:242–44, for R. le Tardif); in 1433, the university appealed against the bailiff of Rouen, who had taken prisoner several university members at Rouen (Denifle and Chatelain, eds., Chartularium, vol. 4, no. 2425). All these instances are carefully studied in P. Kibre, Scholarly Privileges in the Middle Ages (London, 1961), particularly chap. 6, pp. 179–226.

The university did not remain passive before these abuses, and things got settled quietly as a rule; despite a few threats to do so, the university never had to suspend its lectures or examinations. Yet, these incidents prevented a greater confidence between government and university, and they show how anxious the royal power was to keep the university obedient and its autonomy within bounds. A more serious incident took place in the last years of Anglo-Burgundian rule, when the English created the university at Caen (January 1432). [25] This decision revealed Bedford's calculations; foreseeing the breakdown of the double monarchy and the reversal of the alliance of Philip the Good, he was resigned to concentrating the English occupation in the duchy of Normandy. The creation of the university at Caen ruined the confidence of the university men at Paris in the double monarchy: it was a threat to the enrollment of students and a sting to their professional pride in so far as the English seemed to consider them as no more than the university for Paris and its neighborhood.

One has to bear in mind all these factors, as well as the constant aspiration to peace, before trying to explain the apparent volte-face of the university men in 1435. In August of that year, after some preparatory negotiations, representatives of the King of England, of Charles VII, and the Duke of Burgundy convened at Arras. With the Burgundians were associated, among others, the delegates of the University of Paris, headed by Thomas de Courcelles, a doctor of theology. The negotiations were difficult, and on 1 September the English broke up the talks and left Arras, resolved to continue the armed struggle. Philip the Good then decided to abandon his old allies and disavow the double monarchy, the birth of which he had favored fifteen years earlier. Through certain territorial concessions and reparation for the murder of John the Fearless, he made peace with Charles VII and recognized him as the only legitimate king of France. This was a decisive turn in the Hundred Years' War, for the English would henceforth have to oppose Charles VII's reconquest alone,

[25] Cf. M. de Boüard, "Quelques données nouvelles sur la création de l'Université de Caen (1432–1436)," in *Le Moyen-Age*, anniversary issue (1963), pp. 727–41.

without any help within the country. During the negotiations the delegates of the university were among the most enthusiastic advocates of this reconciliation of the Duke of Burgundy with Charles VII. *Le Journal de la Paix d'Arras* tells us that Thomas de Courcelles, who shortly before had been one of the most ferocious of the judges of Joan of Arc, put forth this position in a speech, with great effort.[26] According to him, the reconciliation of the houses of France and of Burgundy would make it possible to bring to the realm the general peace which had been sought in vain for so long.

A year later, on 13 April 1436, the French forces captured Paris. Not many doctors had fled to the English camp for shelter, and the great majority of the university community transferred its allegiance to Charles VII. The King proclaimed a general amnesty and confirmed the privileges of the university in such laudatory terms that one might have thought nothing had changed.[27] The doctors, in return, staged processions and masses and in their letters extolled "the wonderful sudden submission of your majesty's goodly city of Paris" and "the sincere love of the people for their natural lord and liege" so manifest in all those subjects now returned to a "most desired obedience" to the French sovereign.[28]

The honeymoon was short-lived. There were too many elements in Charles VII's policies that were uncongenial to the university, but its protests went unheeded. At the Estates General at Orléans, in 1439, the university complained that the war was dragging on and asked for an immediate compromise peace with the English or at least a truce.[29] It did not seem to it that the total liberation of the national territory deserved so many sacrifices. Moreover, the Church policy symbolized by the Pragmatic Sanction (1438) was a cause of worry: would not the local collators be less generous than the popes in apportioning benefices to the university? Hence at the assemblies of the Church of France that met between 1440 and 1450, the university men asked for

[26] Cf. Antoine de la Taverne, *Journal de la Paix d'Arras*, published by A. Bossuat (Paris, 1936), particularly pp. 63–68.
[27] Denifle and Chatelain, eds., *Chartularium*, vol. 4, nos. 2485–86.
[28] *Ibid.*, nos. 2481, 2483.
[29] *Ibid.*, no. 2536.

new negotiations with Rome in order to agree on a true concordat.[30]

Above all, the university had to face the increasing hostility of the state. Not only was it denied any political initiative, but even its privileges and autonomy were under attack. Willingly or not, the university would have to become an instrument devoted to the service of the state. From 1436 to 1450 there are many indications of this strife. Trials became more frequent because of the many abuses committed by the King's agents,[31] and we see the Parlement itself and the royal prosecutors becoming more and more hostile to the university franchises. The letters and embassies sent to Charles VII denouncing this situation got an increasingly unfavorable reception.[32] Finally, the university had to resort to its time-honored weapon: strike (*cessatio*). In the years 1441 to 1446, five strikes brought the university to a standstill for a third of the time.[33] All this was of no avail: Charles VII's government was all-powerful against a helpless university. On 26 March 1446, with the extension of the Parlement's jurisdiction to all the civil cases of the university,[34] its chief privilege was abolished and its independence taken away, destroying its ability to play an effective political role.

In brief, this was the role played by the University of Paris from 1418 to 1450—its main interventions in public affairs and its relations with the English and then with the French authorities. We cannot content ourselves with this review, however, because it simply shows the university adopting the same attitudes as the other supporters of the Burgundians in Paris. What is of interest is the originality of those attitudes in so far as they reveal the political outlook of the university.

We must therefore assess what were the abiding preoccupa-

[30] Cf. N. Valois, *Histoire de la pragmatique sanction de Bourges sous Charles VII* (Paris, 1906).

[31] For instance, Denifle and Chatelain, eds., *Chartularium*, nos. 2501, 2551, 2602; *Matinées*, X1A 4801, fol. 57.

[32] For instance, Denifle and Chatelain, eds., *Chartularium*, nos. 2586, 2591, 2592, 2615, 2658, 2699, etc.

[33] *Ibid.*, nos. 2553, 2569, 2579, 2607; Tuetey, ed., *Journal d'un bourgeois de Paris*, pp. 375–76.

[34] Denifle and Chatelain, eds., *Chartularium*, vol. 4, no. 2608.

tions of the university despite changing circumstances and apparently shifting attitudes. It would seem that throughout the period under consideration it assigned itself a few definite objectives which are worth studying in themselves because they illustrate its conception of its rank and role in French society.

Foremost among these objectives was the defense of its privileges, which may not seem a strictly political aim, although it certainly was for those concerned. We must remember that in the Middle Ages the privileges of the university or any similar corporation were not special advantages but were the very conditions of existence: they were what made such bodies autonomous, with their own rules and rights, among the other institutions of the realm. Now in the fifteenth century these privileges and the almost absolute autonomy they conferred upon the university were called into question more and more openly. Consequently, the university had to stand up for them and in so doing felt that it was protecting its very existence. Its traditional prestige and widespread influence—indeed, the proper accomplishment of its mission—were essentially dependent on its autonomy and traditional privileges. As their defense proved more and more difficult in that period, the university had to make dangerous concessions in order to preserve what seemed essential. The most instructive documents in this respect are the records of the lawsuits brought by the university before the Parlement in protest against several violations of its privileges.

There were two ways of looking at the privileges of the university and their legal and political status within the general organization of the realm. The more traditional view is that of the university as an age-old institution (here we may recall the theme of *translatio studii*[35]) or, at any rate, one Christian in origin. It owed

[35] It was a mythical reconstitution of the history of the University of Paris that placed its origins even before the Christian era, in ancient Egypt. From there, following the general evolution of civilization, the university was presumably transferred to Athens, then to Rome, and finally to Paris. This traditional theme was still being sounded in the fifteenth century by university men when they wanted to establish the independence of the university vis-à-vis any particular political power (for example, in a letter of 1418: "dès le commencement de ce siècle [avons] esté en noz prédécesseurs premiérement en Egipte, après en Athènes puis à Romme et desrainnement en ceste bonne ville de Paris" [*ibid.*, no. 2120]).

its privileges to the popes and the emperors (hence the frequent references to the Authentic *Habita*[36]); they were therefore outside the jurisdiction of the kings of France, situated on a universal plane and impossible to abrogate without raising a conflict with the Church. A text dated 1432 says: "The privileges of the university are, for the large part, pontifical privileges, granted by the pope whom every Catholic is bound to obey."[37] This thesis had become suspect by the fifteenth century, and the university men themselves seldom referred to it, or, if they did, it was without much conviction. Before the Parlement the king's prosecutors formally denounced it and refused to see in the privileges of the university anything but a royal concession; the exercise of these privileges ought to be controlled by the king's justice, they said, and every abuse, every attempt to place the university beyond the reach of the common law of the realm, ought to be punished. Let us quote a few entries in the records of the Parlement, remembering, of course, that the hostility of the royal power to the privileges of the university was noticeable before 1436. In 1427, a Burgundian prosecutor replied to the delegates of the university that they must "let the king exercise his justice and must not desire anything so much as seeing this justice done . . . ; therefore, they must not oppose the justice of the king nor say, 'we have privileges and will not show them.' "[38] And further on, "The king has not granted privileges against himself but against private persons . . . and a privilege cannot extend against the king, for the very reason that a privilege is against common law."[39] In 1446, a prosecutor of Charles VII spoke in very much the same terms: "To the king in his kingdom, where he is emperor and not

[36] Cf. Chapter 1 of this volume, p. 32.

[37] Denifle and Chatelain, eds., *Chartularium*, no. 2192: "privilegia Universitatis pro majori parte sunt papalia et concessa a summis pontificibus, quibus quilibet catholicus tenetur obedire."

[38] The University of Paris must "laissier le roy user de sa justice et ne doivent rien tant désirer fors que justice soit faite . . . ; pour ce, ne doit empeschier la justice du roy ne dire: nous avons privilèges et ne les monstrerons point" (20 June 1427; *Matinées*, X1A 4795, fol. 114).

[39] "Et n'a pas le roy donné privilèges contre lui mais contre privéez personnes" (21 July 1427); "et ne s'extendera point le privilège contre le roy, mesmement pour ce que le privilège est contre droit commun" (August 1427; *ibid.*, fols. 128v, 160v).

subject to any man, it belongs—and not to the pope or any other —to create corporate bodies. He has created the university and endowed it with privileges, as was meet. And the university is his daughter, bound to him in reverence, honor, and subjection."[40] The royal prosecutors were especially fierce in attacking the right to strike, which for them was an inadmissible license for disobedience and even rebellion: the university was only to contribute to the orderly management of the realm, and was to trust the king to ensure its means of living.[41]

The university men during this period faced such attacks with flexibility. They refrained from invoking the supranational origin of their privileges and were content to consider them as royal concessions, while stressing that these privileges, necessary to the normal organization of studies, were by no means a threat to the king's sovereignty but were part and parcel—along with the privileges of all the other corporate bodies of the realm—of the common law invoked by his prosecutors. Now, if the king was not a tyrant, he was in duty bound to respect the privileges he had himself granted.

Let us offer a few more quotations. In 1436, the university acclaimed the capture of Paris by Charles VII's army and entreated the King to "maintain, preserve and favor the university in all the privileges that had been granted to it by the king's predecessors and, indeed, to increase and develop them most graciously as a testimony of his fatherly affection."[42] As early as

---

[40] "Au roy en son royaume, car il y est empereur et non sugect à homme, appartient seul, et non à Pape, ne autre, créer corps ne commune. Il a créé le corps de l'Université et grandement privilégié, et c'est bien raison, et est l'Université sa fille; ainsi lui doit révérence, honneur et subjection" (*Matinées*, XIA 4801, fol. 57v).

[41] The royal ordinance of 1446 that turned over to the Parlement all civil cases of the university began by denouncing this excessive usage of the right to strike: "ceux de la dicte Université, en grand contempt et mespris de nous et de nostre dicte justice souveraine et des dictes defenses et commandemens, en mesprenant contre nous grandement, ont cessé et fair cesser de prédicacions et faire sermons au peuple de la parole de Dieu, qui est contre raison" (Denifle and Chatelain, eds., *Chartularium*, no. 2608).

[42] "(. . . supplicetur regie majestati ut) nostram Universitatem in suis privilegiis, que a suis progenitoribus concessa sunt, manutenere, conservare et favere, illaque augere et ampliare paterno dignetur affectu" (27–30 April 1436; *ibid.*, no. 2483).

1426 an advocate of the university said: "The privileges are not directed against the king. . . . He has willingly entered a bond with the university for the sake of the general good and the public utility; it is then not such a matter of privileges as of common law . . . and it is unlikely that the king would wish to worry and disturb the scholars, as he forbids others to cause them any worry."[43]

It is, of course, in this perspective that the theme of the University of Paris being the eldest daughter of the king of France should be seen. Nicolas Midi, in the speech already mentioned, said to the young Henry VI as he entered Paris: "The king is the father, the patron, and the special protector of the university, which is our sovereign lord's eldest daughter."[44] This text shows very well that the university was looking to the king essentially for protection and favors.

If I have dwelt on this nonpolitical problem of the privileges, it is because of its importance for the university itself. This was its constant concern, all the more acute as the political situation became more serious and fraught with menace. One understands why in these circumstances the university had to be pliable and docile in its relations with the established authorities. In those days, whether it was English or French, the state was evolving in the direction of centralization and absolutism. It claimed control over the exercise of private privileges in the kingdom and also, as we shall see later, over the mode of attributing Church benefices, which were the main source of the university's revenue. At this point the university could no longer afford, as it had in the thirteenth century, to set itself openly against the royal power because that would have been suicidal. A certain measure of agreement with the government was necessary for proper functioning. The Anglo-Burgundians were, no doubt,

---

[43] "Ne sont mie les privilèges contre le roy. . . . Le roy s'est bien voulu lié au privilège de l'Université pour l'utilité et le bien publique et n'est mie *simpliciter* privilèges mais est de droit commun . . . , et n'est mie vraisemblable que le roy veulle inquiéter et distraire lez escoliers de leur estude, qui défend que lez autres ne les inquiétent" (*Matinées*, X1A 4795, fols. 160–61).

[44] "Ipse [Henricus VI] est pater, patronus et tutor singulareque refugium dicte Universitatis, que est dicti domini nostri regis filia primogenita" (Denifle and Chatelain, eds., *Chartularium*, vol. 4, no. 2399).

more generous than Charles VII, and the university endured their supervision more easily; yet before as well as after 1436 the relative position was much the same—a weak university and an increasingly ambitious and authoritarian Crown.

The problem of the privileges led to the political dependency and inefficiency of the university, and the situation could only have been aggravated by the vision which the university men had of political problems as such. We should note that their only strictly political aim throughout that period was the immediate return to peace. They no longer put forward, as in a preceding age, any general theory of power or government; instead, they always sided, whatever party they belonged to, with the more pacifist wing: through letters and delegations they kept insisting on the urgency of restoring peace and proposed several plans to this effect.

In 1418 they accused the Orléanists of deliberately pursuing the war to strengthen their own power.[45] In 1420 they participated in the formulation of the Treaty of Troyes. In 1431 they accused Joan of Arc of rekindling war while the country could have lived in peace. This pacifism also explains the volte-face in 1435: since the English were proving unable to establish a lasting peace, the university would ask it from Charles VII; its role at the Arras conference and its transfer of loyalty to Charles VII was based on the fact that the French reconquest seemed to promise an early peace settlement. But, with the war dragging on, the university soon had to sue for immediate peace negotiations, which it did at the Estates General of Orléans in 1439 and in the following years.

This being the situation, we may ask ourselves how the university men imagined the return to peace and why their plans proved so futile in the end: peace was restored, but only in 1453 and not at all along the lines they had recommended. Their reasoning was simple, or rather oversimple and too abstract. On the one hand, war was considered as an absolute evil. Nowhere do

---

[45] "Illud enim erat gravius quod, dum de pace nollent agi [Arminiaci] et nomen pacis per se ipsum dulce naturaque cunctis acceptabile cognoscerent, pacis desiderium simulantes, odiosas condiciones pacis tractatibus inserebant, ne cunctis mortalibus optanda pax oriretur" (*ibid.*, no. 2107).

we find the classic theme of the "just war," known in canon law as a defensive war, fought against aggression or rebellion, and for legitimate ends. In our texts, the war is always viewed as the occasion of all disasters: the material disasters were described in general terms as the depopulation of the land, the ruin of the economy, and brigandry; the spiritual disasters were the decline of worship, of education, and of religious faith. All men shared in that sinful condition as criminals or their accomplices. When Christians fought one another the difference between civil and foreign war was insignificant because in the end the victim was Christendom.[46] On the other hand, peace was necessarily endowed with every blessing and virtue: it was an absolute good, giving back prosperity to the kingdom, calm to conscience, and ascendancy to the faith; in peace Christian men were united in one congregation.[47] For the university men peace was therefore an essentially religious reality, the return to the good order of Christian society which enabled men to ensure their material existence and, above all, their salvation. The restoration of peace was then a matter of good will, of spiritual conversion and religious zeal.[48] The Church was called on to play an eminent role in

[46] Cf. the description of the horrors of war in the instructions given by the university to its delegates to the conference at Arras: "Poterunt ibidem multa dici de desolatione hujus regni, de destructione et principium et milicie et ecclesiarum ac populorum, multitudine scelerum, perpetracione omnium malorum, destructione et intermissione omnium bonorum; . . . timendum [est] ne omnes fere conscientie hominum, et majorum et minorum, qui vel ista perpetrant, vel non puniunt, aut non corrigunt, vel dissimulant, gravissimis peccatis coram Deo pollute inveniantur" (*ibid.*, no. 2462).

[47] In 1439, at the Estates General in Orléans, the university delegates pointed out "bona consequencia pacis, que sunt reparacio et augmentacio divini cultus, reconciliacio fidelium ad Deum et ad proximum; restauracio templorum et locorum piorum; populi multiplicacio, agriculture et mercanciarum cursus, viarum securitas et populacio regni, civitatum et studiorum, cum universa dictorum inconveniencium, tyrannidum et iniquitatum sedacione et extirpacione" (*ibid.*, no. 2536).

[48] One can find an instance of this religious definition of peace in the instructions given to the university delegates at Arras in 1435: "Principes pacatos, clerum in transquillitate Deo servientem, populum cum pace viventem, unumcumque, ut Scriptura loquitur, sub vite sua et sub ficu sua, si pro odiis et inimicitiis caritatem et concordiam, pro invidia gratiam, pro omnibus sceleribus omnem virtutem, pro summa egestate opes, divitias et omnium bonorum copiam, Deo largiente et ipsis [principibus] adjuventibus, catholicus populus assequeretur" (*ibid.*, no. 2462).

this enterprise and, in particular, the University of Paris, which considered itself to be the fount of all knowledge within the Church and to be invested with an unequalled authority. A passage from the text presented by the deputies of the university to the Arras conference in 1435 shows this very clearly: "It is the mission of our Holy Mother the Church to preach concord to her divided sons; it devolves upon her to lead them to a most desirable peace, to pursue crime, to define and realize all the contributes to the salvation of souls, the exaltation of the Catholic faith and Christian religion, and to the unity of the people of God."[49] Everything in this text is strictly religious. The university seemed to overlook the fact that a treaty of peace has to be negotiated in a given political context and must take into account the strength of the adversaries, their respective ambitions, the state of public opinion, and economic factors. All this requires fairly precise information and analysis (not beyond the capacity of a fifteenth-century government), but the university men preferred abstract formulas and religious schemes, both sublime and oversimplified, which reduced their stance to an unrealistic and impotent one.

Two examples will serve to illustrate this point. From 1420 to approximately 1432 the university was a staunch supporter of the double monarchy system established by the Treaty of Troyes. It seemed an excellent peaceful solution because, in uniting under the same monarch two peoples hitherto separated, it did away with a permanent cause of division of the Christian people and of war. Nicolas Midi expressed this view to Henry VI in 1431: "This is the beginning of a great felicity for Christendom, for two kingdoms are now united that used to be divided and inimical, so that wars, conflicts, seditions, the ruin of many churches and the decline of worship were the results. . . . But henceforward, thanks to the union brought about by the grace of

---

[49] "Ad sanctam matrem Ecclesiam pertinet filios suos dissidentes in concordiam revocare et ad pacem jugiter confovendam omni diligentia et studio suadere et inducere, scelera prohibere et ea annunciare ac prosequi que sunt ad salutem animarium et exaltacionem fidei catholice et christianissime religionis et plebis christiane unitatem et transquillitatem" (*ibid.*, no. 2462).

God, all those evils will cease; this is what we now hope for."[50]
The theoretical position of the university could hardly be more
explicit, but it obviously disregarded the political obstacles which
rendered the system of the double monarchy almost inapplicable.
It ignored the risks of colonizing France by the English aristocracy, the force of national feelings in both countries, and the
nascent French patriotism made manifest in the attachment of
the people to Charles VII.

Now for our second illustration. In the years 1432 to 1435, the
university had to face the facts: the double monarchy was
doomed, and something else had to be found as a means of restoring peace. The doctors then presumed to submit to both governments their plans for division of the kingdom on the basis of the
territorial status quo. As early as 1432 they suggested that peace
could be achieved without delay if Charles VII were allowed to
keep all the provinces he actually controlled south of the Loire.[51]
After 1436 they proposed to Charles VII a similar solution: at
the Estates General of Orléans in 1439 they urged him to be
reconciled at once with the English by letting them dispose of
the areas they still occupied in Normandy and Guyenne.[52] Again,
as we can see, pacifism at all costs overrode practical considerations. As though everything were a pure question of good will,
the university men did not reckon with the claims of the crowns
of France and England, the ambitions of the princes, or the force
of the popular support for Charles VII's effort of national liberation. They did not suspect that neither the governments involved
nor public opinion in France would have accepted a partition of
the kingdom and the resignation of sovereignty which they suggested with such equanimity.

In fact, the pacifism of the university must be seen from a more
comprehensive viewpoint; otherwise it might be ascribed to politi-

---

[50] "Excellens bonum pro Christianitate est inchoatum, in quo due regna
sunt unita, que prius fuerunt divisa et discordantia, unde guerre, bella, sedi-
tiones, ecclesiarum ruine et cultus diminutio acciderunt; nunc autem, per hanc
unionem in eo factam, per Dei gratiam, omnia mala cessabunt, sicuti speran-
dum est" (*ibid.*, no. 2399).
[51] *Ibid.*, no. 2420.
[52] *Ibid.*, no. 2536.

cal naïveté and lack of realism without due attention to the general conception which explains it. The university in that period did not attempt to play a political role in the modern sense of the phrase. Its public vocation was above all religious, and its mission was the defense of Christian values whenever they were in danger. This paramount objective is sufficient, in my opinion, to explain in every detail the role of the University of Paris at the close of the Hundred Years' War.

We have just analyzed the pacifism of the university and have seen that the peace it so much talked about was conceived as an eminently Christian value and not a political reality determined by a set of circumstances. Another classic example is the trial of Joan of Arc. Here the intervention of the university was justified as an attempt to protect Christian faith from a threat. It did not level any political accusations against Joan, only religious arguments: she was guilty of disturbing the peace of the Christian people, she was a witch, a heretic, and a false prophet undermining the authority of the Church and leading souls to their perdition.[53] This is why the university, "light of all science," felt entitled to set itself against her. And there is no reason to think that most of the doctors were not acting in good faith. For them the political aspect of her mission was merely the consequence of her religious errors, and those indeed had to be condemned.

This interpretation seems to be confirmed by the frequent allusion to the theme of the "most Christian kingdom of France." It was a corollary to the principle by which the university conceived its political function and was quite in the tradition of Augustinian politics: princes in general, and the "most Christian king of France" in particular, had one essential mission, and that was to further the unity, the security and the glory of the Church.[54] The university as the unrivaled religious authority in

[53] The university's attitude is well summed up in this sentence we can read in a letter sent to Bishop Cauchon (13 May 1431): "Per cujus [i.e., Johanne] latissime dispersum virus ovile christianissimum totius fere occidentalis orbis infectum manifestatur" (P. Champion, ed., *Procès de condamnation de Jeanne d'Arc* [Paris, 1920], vol. 1: *Texte Latin*, p. 358).

[54] At the Council of Bourges (1438), the university delegates asserted that: "teste Isidoro, infra Ecclesiam seculi potestates necssarie non essent nisi quod non praevalent sacerdotes efficere per doctrine sermonem, potestas hoc imperet per discipline terrorem" (Du Boulay, *Historia*, 5:443–45).

the kingdom had the right and the duty to counsel the king on such matters. Some deputies of the university declared before the Parlement, in 1444: "His majesty the king is the head of the temporal jurisdiction in his kingdom; his daughter, the university, means to assist, advise, and support him in all that relates to religion."[55] This claim seemed perfectly legitimate to the Parisian doctors, and nobody sought to deny it, at least officially. Neither the popes nor the kings of France would oppose it. Charles VII himself said in 1436 that "he bore the university a great and fervent love" because he trusted that the "precious fruits his predecessors had known to accrue from the university to their crown, kingdom, and seigniory" would now be his to enjoy.[56] He himself caused the university to take part in the Process in Rehabilitation of Joan of Arc (1450–56), thus demonstrating that he recognized its religious competence and even its right to extend that authority to political affairs.

We see that the outlook of the university was the one that had developed some thirty years before at the time of the Schism and the Councils but now was transferred to the national plane. The university saw itself as above all a religious authority, operating within the limits of Christendom. France was merely a sector of this field of activity and politics something to be carried on in the light of religious principles. This was a very consistent position, admittedly, but one running contrary to the new trends of French civilization in the fifteenth century. These new trends were the affirmation of the state, the awakening of national consciousness and a lay spirit, and the evolution of politics from ethics and religion to technique or craft in its own right. It may be said of our doctors that they lacked true political sense, resisting or rather failing to grasp the implications of modern politics, and they were therefore condemned to inefficiency and gradual effacement as a social force.

[55] "Le roy nostre sire est le chef de la juridiction temporelle *in regno suo;* . . . *Universitas ejus filia* le y veult aidier, advertir et favoriser en ce mesmes qui regarde la foy" (Denifle and Chatelain, eds., *Chartularium,* vol. 4, no. 2581).

[56] "Les autres prècieux fruis et biens qu'ils ont perceu et sentu si largement et grandement yssir et venir d'ella à nostre couronne, royaume et seigneurie" (*ibid.,* no. 2486).

The last topic examined here will be the "why" of this attitude. We shall recall some of the material and social conditions of the university men which may have been determining factors. We must also take into account the collective mentality underlying their behavior which gave it its own psychology and caused the lasting divergences between the university and the age.

Let it be said at the start that only a few tentative hypotheses can be offered. In order to interpret with any degree of certainty the political attitudes of the university, a thorough study of its social structure, of the educational organization, of the incomes of its members, and, perhaps, of their personal quarrels would be required. In the absence of such a study, we shall have to be content with a few impressions suggested by the evidence from the *Chartularium*.

Some explanation may be found in the physical situation of the university. First of all, its geographic base in northern France became much more evident in the fifteenth than in the thirteenth and fourteenth centuries. Owing to the Schism and the war, foreign students had become less numerous.[57] Most university staff members were natives of northern France; they were attached to Paris and felt closer to the people there. Many students belonged to colleges where the conditions of life were more stable. A massive exodus of the university community from the town, as in the thirteenth century, was out of the question because of these material and psychological reasons.[58] The doctors became integrated into the class of Parisian worthies, so that the university could not very easily remain immune to the great currents of opinion in contemporary Paris, even if it gave them its particular imprint. On the other hand, as it became more closely associated with the town, it was more susceptible to government pressure.

Let us now turn to the question of incomes. Most teachers and students drew their incomes essentially from the benefices devolv-

[57] Cf. A.-L. Gabriel, "Les Étudiants étrangers à l'Université de Paris au XVe siècle," *Annales de l'Université de Paris*, no. 3 (1959), pp. 377–400.

[58] One can very often find such expressive sentences as this: the university delegates say that "locum studiis quam Parisius non esse sub celo apriotem" (January 1451; Denifle and Chatelain, eds., *Auctarium*, vol. 2, col. 841).

ing on parish priests and canons. The close study of the geographic distribution of these benefices would of course enlighten us, yet it already appears from the information supplied by the existing sources that Normandy, not surprisingly, was of great importance in this respect. The Anglo-Burgundians after 1418 presented their friends in the university with many benefices situated in Normandy, which was a place safer than many others. It is beyond doubt that the situation in Normandy dictated to some extent the political attitudes of the university men. It led them at first to support the double monarchy because it was favorable to the papal mode of conferring benefices and did away with any risk of political separation between Paris and that province. But after 1432, with the creation of the University of Caen and the French reconquest of Normandy, which turned the area into a battleground and depleted revenues, the university went over to Charles VII, hoping that he would pacify the whole province and restore the totality of their resources to the doctors. They expected him, furthermore, to abolish the "*studiolum*" created by the English at Caen. Yet those hopes were slow to be realized, and the university men soon lost their confidence in Charles. In 1439, as was noted above, they suggested the negotiation of truces to put an end to the strife, especially in Normandy. The province, of course, would remain an English possession, but this did not matter so long as the university men were granted their request and, although residing in Paris, were allowed to collect the revenues from their benefices in Normandy.

We could go on with this analysis, yet it will be sufficient to bear in mind that the university in the fifteenth century, because of its geographical implantation, became more vulnerable and more subservient to government pressure, that its material interests took on a greater importance and, naturally enough, determined that unfailing pacifism previously described.

Another aspect of the social and material situation of the university between 1420 and 1450 should be emphasized. Since precise data are not available, we shall not go into the subject in detail, yet, since so many indications point to it, we cannot fail to take into consideration the serious difficulties, if not, indeed, a general crisis, within the university. No doubt the complaints about the crisis are often exaggerated in the texts,[59] yet it seems certain that in this period the number of students declined, many of them leaving Paris before they had completed their course of studies. The incomes of the colleges and the doctors decreased, and hence there was an erratic organization of teaching and a lowering of quality. Many regents, moreover, were often on leave of absence so that they could take part in political conferences and debates, either as delegates of the university or on their personal behalf.[60] There were also some cases of voluntary exile or of purge in 1418 and again in 1436, although only a few individuals were affected. These considerations might be expanded upon, but we shall focus mainly on one aspect of the situation, namely, the necessity for the university, as it faced a potential crisis, to defend its privileges.

The crisis made the university still more impotent against the authorities, who might have exploited the situation to bring about the ruination of the university had it given some sign of genuine independence. Finally, we should also point out that the difficulties and disorganization were largely the result of the war and could only reinforce the pacifist tendency of the university men. With few exceptions, they had nothing to gain from the

[59] For instance, at the beginning of 1419 the university wrote to Charles VI, "La dicte vostre fille [the University] est en voie d'estre tout dissipée et désolée" (Denifle and Chatelain, eds., *Chartularium*, no. 2134), and in 1421, to the Duke of Burgundy, "Actum erit de nobis et cito irreparabiliter extinctum nomen Universitatis studii Parisiensis, in quantam jacturam regni, vos ipse videritis, inclite princeps" (*ibid.*, no. 2180). In 1426, in letters sent to Pope Martin V, the University complained about "beneficiorum tenuitatem et suppositorum ejusdem Universitatis plurimorum paupertatem" (21 December; *ibid.*, no. 2289) and said: "Sat passi sumus, supra modum sparsi et, quod dolenter referimus, a veteri gloria nostra, ymo vestra imminuti" (26 February; *ibid.*, no. 2250).

[60] One finds the same phenomenon in the other European universities at this time. At the very moment when they began to play an active political role their value as teaching and research institutions declined as a result of the departure of students frightened by the troubles accompanying this political activity and the growing absenteeism of the masters—thus it was at Oxford at the time of the Wyclifite disturbances or at Prague at the time of the Hussites (see Chapter 3 of this volume).

continuation of the war: only with peace would students, revenues, and scholarly tranquillity return.

We have examined some factors that might help interpret the
political attitudes of the University of Paris at the end of the
Hundred Years' War. But they are not sufficient. We must also
consider the psychology of the university people. These psychological factors at times appear to work in the selfish interests of
the university, but in other circumstances they achieve a true
autonomy. In any case, the doctors certainly had a general conception of society and their place within it which, although it had
become unconscious in many cases, must have determined their
political attitudes and cast them into a coherent pattern.

Let us now present a draft of this general conception, although
it is provisional and is open to criticism and correction. Roughly
speaking, it seems that the university men conceived of the organization of society as revolving about two poles. In the first
place, there was the university, an autonomous and self-sufficient
institution which remained for many doctors the *Alma Mater*, the
necessary surrounding for lives amost entirely given up to scholarly work. We could observe the same attitude in other European
universities in this period—for example, as Professor Kaminsky
shows in his essay in this volume, at Prague in the age of the
Hussite Revolution one can find among the leading Czech
masters of arts the same professional solidarity, the same acute
sense of the material interests of the university, which is in fact
at the root of their interventions in the political affairs of the
country. This had an influence upon social and political attitudes. The primacy of the corporate framework results in collective selfishness and narrowmindedness; the university would
cover up the private actions of some of its members, whatever
they might be. It was always ready to strike a compromise or
give in to the petty exactions of the authorities when its survival
was at stake. The university was for its members a time-honored
institution situated far above warring factions. But seen from the
outside, the picture was not the same. In the government and the
public view the political unsteadiness of the university did not

reflect accidental variations but was taken as a sure sign of its decline and vulnerability. Moreover, this tendency to professional pride could easily degenerate into simple blindness to the facts, so that it was easy to coax the university into supporting this party or that (a game at which John the Fearless was expert), or to arouse its vindictiveness against those, like Joan of Arc, who failed to recognize, or denied, the doctrinal supremacy it claimed.

The university men extended their gaze beyond the limits of the university to Christendom itself, which was the other pole around which they saw society revolving. For them it was a flesh-and-blood reality, defined as the equilibrium of a society turned towards religious goals, in which princes were the servants of the Church and the Church the teacher and defender of those Christian values which enabled man to direct his life upon earth and to prepare for his salvation—and of course the University of Paris was, within the Church, the shining light of knowledge and faith. The period of the Great Schism had revivified these themes, and it is not surprising to see the university men perceiving above all the religious problems concealed in the political events of the time. These were the classic ones of upholding the faith, the peace, and the liberties of the Church (which meant in this case the privileges of the university). Likewise, the problems of French society were seen as calling for theoretical solutions of a religious character, dependent on a total vision of things. But this vision was old-fashioned and without much relevance to the problems and aspirations of the contemporary world.

Engrossed as they were in the contemplation of these two visionary poles, the university men were rather insensitive to the nascent feeling of nationalism. They did not ignore it altogether: they could express, upon request, the ideas relating to the state or patriotism in very much the same language as most other people of the time. Let us look at the letter written in December 1418 by the university in support of the besieged city of Rouen. With the aim of arousing a patriotic reaction to a national cause, the letter appeals to loyalty to the Crown and to the solidarity of all the people in the kingdom.[61] The tone would seem fairly genuine were it not remembered that the letter was written at the instigation of John the Fearless and that when he gave up the city, a month later, the university never uttered a word in protest. In fact, the university men had no notion of the modern state, and patriotism was not a passion with them, as we may guess from their attitudes.[62] This is why they so easily accepted the double monarchy and paid no attention to the problems it raised and why they later recommended a partition of the kingdom and a renunciation of sovereignty, providing their privileges and benefices were saved. As they said in 1439: "there is no reason why the Church men and university men should be concerned with the mundane collisions of war."[63] Yet at a time when war did concern everyone, when the nation and the state were gaining a new strength from the very struggle, those who deliberately remained apart from modern trends and could only suggest traditional solutions, those who still believed in an outworn conception

[61] "La bonne ville de Rouen . . . est jà en tel péril de destruction . . . qu'il n'est bon ne loyal qui n'en eust doleur et pitié . . . . Se Rouen est prinse, il n'a membre en ce royaume qui n'en soit débilité. Et pour ce, comme en corps naturel, quant un membre est navré ou bléchié, le sanc et les espoirs de vie de tous les aultres y courent, de quelque prééminence qu'ilz soient; aulsi la force, le sanc, la substance de tous les membres de ce royaume doibt maintenant courir à l'aide de telle ville et encontre les anciens ennemis. . . . Pour quoy vous requérons et prions, sur la bonne amour et loyauté que vous voulés avoir au roy, que en ceste extrême necessité veuliés secourir le roy et le royaume, et non pas tant seulement faire l'aide que le roy nostre père et souverain seigneur vous demande, mais avec ce offrir et emploier corps et biens; par ainsi, acquiterés vos consciences vers Dieu, vers le roy vostre souverain seigneur et le nostre, vers le royaume et vers vos frères qui sont en mortelle affliction" (Denifle and Chatelain, eds., *Chartularium*, no. 2120).

[62] At the same time other universities played a much more positive role on this level. That of Prague in the awakening of the Czech national conscience is discussed in Chapter 3 below, but the conditions at Prague were not entirely the same, and it is especially important to note that it was entirely within the university, which was disturbed by the presence of German masters and students, that the Czech academics first became conscious of their national identity and of the necessity for all Czechs to exalt the interests of their country and defend them against foreigners. Thus even at Prague the corporate dimension undoubtedly preceded the national dimension in the conscience of university men.

[63] "Cum . . . ymo ipsi Ecclesie et Universitatis alumpni tali notorie immunitate gaudere debeant, quod nullo jure inter guerrarum prophanos amplexus debeant comprehendi" (*ibid.*, no. 2592).

of society, were condemning themselves to idealism, impotence
and decline.

This theory calls for some minor qualifications, however. Th
traditional conceptions and attitudes we have just dealt with ar
uppermost in official texts and interventions, but if we loo.
closely at some other less formal records, such as the registers o
the Parlement, we come across some statements indicating a sus
ceptibility to modern ideas in some of the doctors. The university
for instance, was indifferent to the nationalist view and t
patriotism because it officially adhered to Christian universal
ism. Yet at the very same time some foreign students were in
volved in litigations with the university before the Parlement
The occasion of these actions at law is immaterial; we shall onl
notice the xenophobia which often aggravated the resentment o
the university against those students: a certain Paul Nicolas,
Hungarian and a bachelor in divinity, had to conduct a lawsui
from 1426 to 1431, when he was in danger of being expelled fron
his college and his nation. "Considering how remote the parts h
come from," the university said, "his obtaining the said degree
might result in several errors and disadvantages to our re
ligion."[64] To which Paul Nicolas retorted that his fellow country
men "were not Saracens . . . but five hundred leagues away fron
them," adding that "his opponents ought not to blame o
slander him even if he came from a very remote land."[65] Were th
doctors in this case so very different from the mass of the people
whose patriotism was to a considerable extent grounded on th
hatred and contempt of the foreigner?

There are other instances of the discrepancy between th
official attitudes of the university and the private feelings o
some doctors in the Process in Rehabilitation of Joan of Arc
Some of those who had been on the bench in 1431 repeated thei

[64] "Pourquoy attendue la grande distance du lieu dont il est, se pourroien
de ce ensuivre plusieurs erreurs et inconvéniens, se il avoit les dits degréz, o
grant préjudice de nostre dicte foy" (Du Boulay, *Historia*, 5:380).

[65] Paul Nicolas says that he "n'est mie d'Esclavonie mais est du pays d
Hongrie et est son pays distant de Paris de V^C lieues et est à V^C lieues de
Sarrasins et fu Saint Martin natif du pais de *Pannonia*; et ne sont point Sarrasin
ne leurs voisins mais les esloingnent de V^C lieues et s'il estoit de loingtain pai
partie adverse ne l'en devroit point blasmer ne injurier" (27 January 1427
Matinées, XIA 4795, fol. 33).

conviction that from a religious point of view Joan had been guilty and that her trial was therefore legitimate,[66] but others admitted they had not acted entirely in good faith, knowing, without daring to say so, that this trial by a religious tribunal was in fact a political machination meant to discredit Charles VII and his supporters. Ysambart de la Pierre said in the plainest terms that "the main reason for staging a religious trial had been to dishonor the King of France."[67]

A last illustration of this point: we have seen that the university did not officially claim any other political right than that of humbly advising the most Christian king of France upon religious matters according to the old tradition of Augustinian politics that presupposes a perfect harmony between spiritual and temporal authorities. Yet a few texts suggest that some university men realized how outdated these theories were and that, from now on, a more modern system was required. If one aimed at advising and controlling the royal authorities, a system of assemblies representative of the "estates" of the realm and sharing with the Crown its responsibility, at least in regard to legal and fiscal matters, was needed. Thus these university men were in touch with a powerful current of opinion that only died out at the close of the fifteenth century, or perhaps in the sixteenth. The university reproached the Orléanists with suppressing the freedom of expression and deliberation of the official assemblies of the realm.[68] In 1433 a representative of the university phrased the following protest against a fiscal ordinance in decidedly parliamentarian style: "Whoever intends to make a law or a constitu-

---

[66] For instance, Jean Beaupère, who even in 1450 maintained that "quant à l'innocence d'icelle Jehanne, elle estoit bien subtille, de subtillité appartenante à femme" (Quicherat, ed., *Procès de condamnation et de réhabilitation de Jeanne d'Arc*, 2:20–21).

[67] "[Dicit] principaliorem causam quare fuit processus sic factus contra eam, [fuisse] ut infamarent regem Francie" (*ibid.*, 2:353).

[68] "Gubernatores isti [i.e., Arminiaci] . . . gravi precepto inhibuerunt ne quid in deliberatione poneretur, et specialiter quod videretur eorum tangere regimen. Sic profecto materiam et deliberandi modum proscipserunt nec veteres congregandi modos permiserunt, nisi prius in sue conspirationis favorem rem agendam cognoscerent. Sic itaque nullus rector habebatur, nisi sue factionis conscius, nihil in deliberatione ponebatur, nisi sue bande consonum; nihil deliberatur quod sua secta concluserat. . . . Omnia tyrannica rabie et coactione vilissime servitutis extorquebantur non solum in nostro studio sed in urbe tota" (9 August 1418; Denifle and Chatelain, eds., *Chartularium*, no. 2107).

tion must in the first place consult those concerned, especially the principal members of the kingdom; how is it that the three estates of this city, and in particular the clergy and university, were not summoned?"[69]

But all this did not go very far; modern attitudes remained marginal. At best they distinguished a few brilliant and open-minded individuals, and in fact they were another reason for the weakness of the university because they undermined the internal cohesion which had been the very foundation of its strength. More generally, it is in this period that some leaders of the university left it in order to make a career in the new centers of power and culture, the Church, the administration, and the households of princes.

But the university as a whole was incapable of adapting itself. It failed to elaborate a new ideology—new social and political concepts—that would have enabled it to grasp the meaning of events and to intervene efficiently. Instead, trying to conceal its impotence and to gratify, at least verbally, its pride of caste, it sought shelter in great traditional themes and in a phraseology whose inanity became ever more evident. This collapse of energy, this verbalism, were also the features of the university's inner life and of its teaching at the close of the Middle Ages. The philosophy of the Schoolmen, which had been so successful in the thirteenth century, was finally degenerating into fantastic speculations.

What we have been able to observe on the political plane is, I believe, but one aspect of a severe and general crisis, that of medieval scholasticism and of the medieval university. Political events no doubt precipitated the crisis, making the decline of the University of Paris more complete and lowering its status in French society, as this essay has attempted to show. But if we hope one day to comprehend the crisis in all its complexity, it is a total investigation of the phenomenon of the fifteenth-century university that we shall have to embark upon.

[69] "Car qui veult faire une loy ou constitucion, il fault appeler ceulx à qui il touche, par espécial les principaulx membres; or est ainsi que en ceste ville a trois Estas, lesquelx, et en espécial les gens d'Eglise et aussi l'Université, n'y ont esté appelléz ne présens" (Tuetey, ed., Clément de Fauquembergue, 3:101–5).

HOWARD KAMINSKY

3 | The University of Prague in the Hussite Revolution: The Role of the Masters

At every point in the course of the Hussite Revolution we meet a group of politicians called "the masters." They are professors in the Arts Faculty of the University of Prague, the band of friends and colleagues that had stood with John Hus and Jerome of Prague in winning Czech control of the formerly German-dominated university and in defending the cause of Wyclifism against the Prague hierarchy and the Roman papacy. In the eyes of the Council of Constance, which ordered the burning of Hus, the masters were "the chief heresiarchs and doctors of the Wyclifite sect, who had destroyed the University of Prague."[1] But in the eyes of their former students, the priests of the revolutionary Taborite wing of Hussitism, they were counter-revolutionaries who used the authority of the university to frustrate the reformation implied by Hus's work. Both views were correct, and we are free to wonder whether Hus himself, had he lived, would have moved to the left along with the movement he had inspired. Nevertheless, the program for which he died on 6 July 1415 was precisely the "Wyclifite" cause, whose continued defense by his

[1] Johannes D. Mansi, ed., *Sacrorum conciliorum nova et amplissima collectio*, vol. 27 (Venice, 1784), col. 1197. I footnote only quotations and major points of scholarly interest, by preference citing the more recent works in major languages. For the rest, the reader is referred to my *A History of the Hussite Revolution* (Berkeley, Calif., 1967) (henceforth cited as *HHR*), which has detailed references to the Czech and other scholarly literature.

colleagues, the masters, made them the irreconcilable enemies of radicalism. In the 1420s, indeed, the main body of masters ever broke with some of their own group, led by Master Jakoubek of Stříbro, whose religious reforms went beyond not only what the Roman Church did accept but what it conceivably could. In the context of reformation and revolution, the masters' insistence on keeping the door open to Rome appears foolish, even bizarre, but Hus himself had taken the same position. It was in fact the men closest to the martyred leader during his life who—except for Jakoubek—were the most conservative Hussites after his death.

Doctor John Jesenic, Hus's lawyer and one of the two or three most important leaders in the old university movement, offers the most striking case. When Jakoubek introduced the practice of giving the laity Communion in the wine, as well as the bread of the Eucharist—"Utraquism," Communion in both kinds— Jesenic at first refused to accept the innovation; when he later did accept it, after it had become a kind of Hussite symbol, he still refused to regard it as necessary to salvation. In 1417 he was the most unyielding of the masters in refusing to make even tactical concessions to radicalism; by 1419, his position was indistinguishable from that of Roman Catholicism except for a loyalty to the cause symbolized by the lay chalice. He died a lonely death in the dungeon of the Catholic Lord Ulrich of Rožmberk because of this loyalty. Master Simon of Tišnov, who stood shoulder to shoulder with Hus in the struggle for Czech control of the university and in the defense of Wyclif, followed a course similar to Jesenic's, except that in 1419 he went all the way back to Rome and next turned up as an anti-Hussite polemicist. Master Christian of Prachatice, the grand old man of the movement, Hus' friend and patron, who had risked his life by going to Constance on Hus's behalf, was not enough of an ideologist to stop being a Hussite, but he tried to ignore virtually every reform carried through by Jakoubek in Prague. Throughout the years of revolution Christian imperturbably chanted the full Latin mass in his church and observed most of the Roman ceremonies that Prague and Tabor alike had scrapped. As for his politics, he was a member

er of the group of extreme reactionaries that was working
ctively for reunion with Rome; like its other members he nar-
owly missed being killed by the Prague mob in 1427 and was
xiled from the city because of his policies. Master Peter of
Mladoňovice also belonged to this group: he had been with Hus
n Constance, had helped both Hus and Jerome there, and had
omposed the hagiographical account of Hus's trial and martyr-
dom that would establish his master's fame throughout Europe.
His next appearance after Constance was as the masters' spokes-
man in condemnation of Taboritism in 1420. This list could be
xtended to include lesser lights—for example, Master Simon of
Rokycany, an associate whom Hus, in one of his last letters from
Constance, greeted as a "friend of truth"; Simon left the movement in 1419 or 1420, and when captured by Žižka's army in
421 he was burnt to death. [2]

The attitudes implied by these rejections and refusals were not
unlike those of Hus in Constance. He accepted Utraquism with
eluctance, never agreeing that it was necessary to salvation, and
his chief practical advice in the matter was to try to get it approved by the Council of Constance or by a future pope. He
ither rejected or moderated the more subversive aspects of the
Wyclifism he had propagated, and in general he went as far as
he could to present his cause as one which was compatible with
he ecclesiastical system of Europe. [3] This was the line taken by
Hus's colleagues after his death; they sought to apply it even in
he most unfavorable circumstances and remained loyal to it
despite much abuse and danger from both the Catholic and
adical-Hussite sides. Their eventual victory, when the Council
of Basel allowed the Hussite realm to rejoin the ecclesiastical order
of Europe, was both incomplete and pyrrhic, but it can be taken
as an indication that the role of the masters was not merely nega-
ive—that they were the proponents of a program relevant to the

[2] For these cases see *HHR*, index; for Peter of Mladoňovice, see Matthew
Spinka, trans., *John Hus at the Council of Constance*, Records of Civilization,
vol. 73 (New York, 1965), pp. 80ff.
[3] Paul De Vooght, *L'Hérésie de Jean Huss* (Louvain, 1960); Matthew Spinka,
John Hus' Concept of the Church (Princeton, N. J., 1966), and *John Hus, a Biography*
(Princeton, N. J., 1968). All these works argue for Hus's essential orthodoxy.
Cf. *HHR*, pp. 53ff., 129ff.

objective possibilities of their situation. It was, in fact, the cause to which they had committed themselves under Hus's leadership in the first decade of the century.

One characteristic of this cause was that it could not find clear definition in the essentially religious terms of discourse imposed by the Hussite reformation after 1415; when the masters had to refer to it they used words like "the truth" or merely let the lay chalice stand for everything. And if we look at their actual activity we find that in fact they never appeared as religious reformers—always excepting Jakoubek of Stříbro—but rather as politicians. In 1414 and 1415, when Jakoubek was introducing Utraquist Communion and the radicals of the provinces were moving towards Waldensianist sectarianism, the masters were chiefly occupied with organizing the Hussite nobility to intervene on Hus's behalf at Constance. After Hus's death at the stake on 6 July 1415, the masters worked with the nobility to create the Hussite League of 5 September, which laid the basis for protection of the "evangelical truth" by the feudality and established the theologians of the University of Prague as the chief authority in all disputed questions of religion. In 1417, when the rise of sectarian radicalism was alienating the feudality, the masters combined with the leading Hussite barons to devise a program for containing the radicals by integrating them into an established Hussite church. Part of the program required the University of Prague to give Utraquism its official sanction, a step the masters had been avoiding for well over a year because of their reluctance to associate the university with a religious novelty condemned by the universal church.

The same structure of political action appears again after the death of King Wenceslas IV in August 1419. A coalition of Hussites—Prague and baronial—drafted a series of demands as conditions on which they would accept as king Emperor Sigismund, Wenceslas's half-brother. The program was pan-Hussite in conception, but at the core was a set of demands designed to give Czechs the first place in the realm, to ensure the use of the Czech language in public affairs, and to reserve the high offices of both church and state to men of Czech nationality. There was also a stipulation that the University of Prague should have final authority in questions of religion.[4] Several months later, after Sigismund had made himself unacceptable, the masters, Praguers, and nobles again joined to procure a king, this time from Poland. The hoped-for king would have to agree to freedom for "all holy truths based on the Bible"—but more concrete provisions were made for confiscation of superfluous clerical property, for the absolute exclusion of Germans and other foreigners from any office in the realm, and for the maintenance of everyone "in his order and estate." To these requirements were tacked on the Four Articles of Prague, a pan-Hussite religious program, but the text of the instructions given to the embassy to Poland indicates that the main emphasis was on the national and political issues, and even on a kind of pan-Slavic appeal to the Poles to help defend the Slavic people from Sigismund and his Germans.[5]

In its negative aspect, the program of the masters and their allies aimed to change the pre-Hussite polity, in which non-Bohemian Germans occupied leading positions in church, state, and society. Its positive goal was a Bohemian *Ständestaat*, or regime of estates, in which the political body would consist of the Czech people led by the Czech estates of the nobility, the towns, and the university.[6] This ideal found remarkable expression in a

---

[4] *HHR*, pp. 296–98.

[5] Václav Novotný, "K otázce polské kandidatury na český trůn," *Sborník Žižkův*, ed. R. Urbánek (Prague, 1924), pp. 131–33.

[6] Many aspects of the terminology of this program have been usefully discussed by Ferdinand Seibt, *Hussitica. Zur Struktur einer Revolution* (Cologne and Graz, 1965), chaps. 3 and 4. I cannot agree that the national ideology in question was nearly as complicated as his analysis of terms makes it out to be. Cf. František Šmahel's more exhaustive collection of passages: "The Idea of the 'Nation' in Hussite Bohemia," *Historica* (Prague) 16 (1969):143–247, 17 (1969):93–197. My picture of the masters projecting the ideal of a Bohemian system of estates, which then necessarily implied *Czech* power and hence found expression in Czech national ideas, disagrees with Seibt's argument that the thrust in question came from the Prague burghers' desire to modify an already existing *Ständestaat* by inserting Prague into the first place in what had been an aristocratic order based exclusively on birth. Šmahel is much more reserved than Seibt in the conclusions he draws from a study of words, but he does identify the university masters behind the Kutná Hora decree as the center of "ideologized nationalism"; the balance subsequently shifted because of the religious emphasis of the wider circles to the left of the masters (*ibid.*, pp. 192f.); my view has much in common with his.

number of literary works composed in 1420 by one of the masters
—probably Laurence of Březová—presenting the Hussite cause
as that of the Czech Crown associated with the city of Prague,
which appears here as the embodiment of the Hussite and
Bohemian realm.[7] In the "Dispute between Prague and Kutná
Hora," the former is presented as a beautiful woman, defending
Hussitism against the Catholic hostility of ugly Kutná Hora
(Kuttenberg), a largely German city. Among many other arguments we find the claim that the Bohemian church should not be
subject to papal government because the latter was derived from
the Donation of Constantine, whose Roman Empire did not then
include Bohemia.[8] Elsewhere, in a work denouncing Sigismund's
coronation as king of Bohemia on 28 July 1420,[9] the rights of the
land are formulated even more pointedly. Sigismund had procured the crown during his temporary occupation of the Prague
castle merely by having the Archbishop of Prague, "a foreigner,"
put it on his head, with the consent of some Catholic barons—a
"furtive coronation," as the "Satire of the Crown of Bohemia"
put it. A crown could be set on an ass in such a way, but the ass
would not be a true king: "Not a coronation, but the unanimous
and canonical election and consent of the towns, barons, and
estates . . . are what institute a prince, king, or ruler." And even
with such an election, the king could not be crowned until he had
sworn "to preserve the rights of his realm and the honor of the
Crown in their integrity" and the estates of the realm in their

[7] The texts have been edited by J. Daňhelka, *Husitské skladby budyšínského
rukopisu* (Prague, 1952); cf. *HHR*, pp. 410, 439f.

[8] Daňhelka, ed., *Husitské skladby*, p. 134. The argument was presumably
inspired by Wyclif's similar point, made several times, that the Pope had no
"dominion" over England because England was not then part of the Empire,
nor had ever been subjected to it, except for a brief time as a result of treachery
and tyranny: see, e.g., *De Potestate Pape*, ed. J. Loserth (London, 1907), pp.
226f. This connection would be an indication that the ideology of the literary
compositions under discussion proceeded from the Wyclifite university circle
rather than simply from the burghers of Prague.

[9] "Corone regni Boemie satira in Regem Hungarie Sigismundum," in
Daňhelka, ed., *Husitské skladby*, pp. 173–78 (the Czech version is "Porok
české koruny . . . ," pp. 32–40).

liberties.[10] This concept of the Crown as an impersonal symbol of the rights of the realm and of the realm's estates—a concept directly derived from contemporary legal thought[11]—is simply the political program of the masters set out in terms of political theory by an author whose membership in Jakoubek's faction and close ties to Prague gave his conceptions a rather special religious flavor, but one who was nevertheless expressing the masters' point of view. Its fundamentally national and political character is expressed in numerous passages, such as the reproach to the Czech barons supporting Sigismund because in doing so they set themselves against not only their own nationality but also the "honor of their land," and the complaint that Sigismund's worst deed, his leading of a crusade against the Czechs, was intended "to exterminate the Czech nationality and settle foreigners in the land."[12] This character contrasts interestingly with the religious and non-national orientation of the University of Paris at this time, as presented by Jacques Verger in the preceding essay. But beneath this contrast, which is real enough, we can see a basic similarity. Both universities had the concept of themselves as

[10] *Ibid.*, p. 173; and pp. 177f.: "Quia non coronacio, sed civitatum, baronum, communitatum unanimis et canonica eleccio pariter et assensus . . . dignum instituunt principem, regem atque rectorem. . . . Iuxta decreta sanctorum patrum rex eciam unanimi et concordi omnium voluntate electus, priusquam diadema susceperit, iurare tenetur iura regni sui et honorem corone illibata servare, iuxtaque legum mearum [*scil.*, of the Bohemian Crown] sancciones coronandus in regem, in publica populi audiencia iuramentum debet manifeste prestare de non obligandis et non alienandis provinciis, civitatibus, castris ad regalis monarchie dicionem quoquomodo spectantibus, et ut barones, clientes, cives et quoslibet terrigenas, quibuscumque nominibus censeantur, in eorum privilegiis, libertatibus, emunitatibus inviolabili stabilitate manutenneat, tueatur et conservet."

[11] The "decreta sanctorum patrum" meant, in concrete terms, the decretal "*Intellecto*" of Pope Honorius III (*Decretales* 2.24.33), from which the phrase "iura regni sui et honorem corone illibata servare" was tacitly and exactly copied. John Jesenic's defense of the Kutná Hora decree in 1409 had cited this decretal: see František Palacký, ed., *Documenta Mag. Joannis Hus vitam, doctrinam, causam . . . illustrantia* (Prague, 1869), pp. 355–63 (*HHR*, pp. 67–69), where "*in collecta*" must be corrected to "*Intellecto*." For the tradition of the ideas involved see the recent survey by Hartmut Hoffman, "Die Unveräusserlichkeit der Kronrechte im Mittelalter," *Deutsches Archiv* 20 (1964):389–474; cf. in general M. Hellman, ed., *Corona regni* (Weimar, 1961).

[12] Daňhelka, ed., *Husitské skladby*, pp. 50, 65.

privileged corporations which made up a part of the political community of the realm, a part specifically qualified to define the norms of public policy and functionally obligated to do so. It was the last gasp of the medieval university before it lost its special status and became merely the kind of training school represented by Christopher Hill's Oxford and Cambridge.

This characterization of the role of the Prague masters poses the problem of the present essay.[13] How did this group of professors become the bearers of the politico-national ideal of a Czech polity? How was that ideal related to the interests of the university as a corporation or to the interests of the professors as individuals? How was it conceptualized or symbolized? How did it come to constitute the selfconsciousness of the masters? And how did it come to acquire the religious dimension which took on a life of its own outside the masters' circle, and which eventually was the basis for the opposition to the masters' program? Some of these questions must be worked out in terms of Hussite history proper in the decade after 1415, but the complex as a whole leads us back into the previous period, when the Czech element at the university was acquiring substance, pushing its way to status and power, and forming the selfconsciousness that validated its thrust. It was in this context that the masters' "cause" took shape—as a program originating in the interests of the Czech academic group but developing religious, political, and national dimensions that went far beyond the immediate concerns of the academy. In the end, the university was sacrificed to the cause. When the Czech minority won control of it in 1409, the German foreigners left. Subsequently, the Law University—a separate organization—ground to a halt, and in 1413, upon the expulsion of its anti-Wyclifite Czech masters, the Theology Faculty disintegrated. In 1417 the Council of Constance suspended the university, thereby ending its existence as far as Europe was concerned, and in Bohemia the turmoil of war made academic functions impossible. Hussitism itself contributed to the decay of the university, for the

[13] Several of the relationships that I study in the following pages have been noted by Ferdinand Seibt in his various essays, but with rather different inferences therefrom; see especially his "Die hussitische Revolution," *Zwischen Frankfurt und Prag* (Munich, 1963), pp. 77f.

secularization of church property in the realm and the abolition of "usurious" rent incomes in Prague cut off most of the ordinary income of the professors. In 1420 the university simply ceased to function at all: although its routine continued from 1423 on, there was very little teaching, and no degrees were granted.[14] What remained was the masters, embodying the program and authority of the old university, which thus survived *only* in its political function. More or less free of the demands of an actual institution, the masters could—indeed had to—pursue their cause to the end, with none of the pacifistic opportunism of their Parisian contemporaries.

The story of how this came to pass begins with the foundation of the University of Prague in 1348 by Charles IV, King of Bohemia and Emperor of the Holy Roman Empire.[15] Like some of his other efforts to raise the status of Bohemia as the center of the Empire, this act had a double significance. Bohemia and its predominantly Czech people were indeed pushed further along the path of development, but at the same time the land was further opened to German foreigners, who predominated at the imperial court, in the prelacies of the Church, and, inevitably, in the university. At first the Czech element in the last institution was of little weight. Through the German students and professors, who came from all parts of the Empire, the university quickly acquired European status as the first such foundation east of France and north of Italy. When the division into "nations" had taken place, by the early 1360s, two nations—the Bavarian and the Saxon—were composed chiefly of German foreigners. A third, the Polish, was soon dominated by Germans from Silesia; only the fourth, the Bohemian, had a Czech majority. University offices were filled on the basis of these divisions, and certain university actions were determined by votes according to nations.

---

[14] W. Tomek, *Geschichte der Prager Universität* (Prague, 1849), pp. 124–27.
[15] For a recent discussion see Miroslav Boháček, "Založení a nejstarší organisace pražské university," *Acta Universitatis Carolinae, Historia Universitatis Carolinae Pragensis* 6 (1965): 5–28 (with a German summary on pp. 29–31). Boháček notes that the first legal founding of the university was effected by Pope Clement VI in his Bull of 26 January 1347; Charles's act of 7 April 1348 represented a second, independent royal foundation, which provided the necessary Bohemian legal status.

Furthermore, when endowed masters' colleges were founded, they too were filled almost wholly by Germans, who chose new members from their own ranks by co-optation. This was the situation when Charles died in 1378, by which time it had already become something of an anomaly. Indeed, Prague was the last of the supra-territorial universities. All those founded in the second half of the fourteenth century were more modest in scope, designed to serve the territorial polities in which they were located by training local church and state officials and by providing princes with councilors and, on occasion, learned authority to support princely policy.[16] Even Paris was losing its supra-national status at this time—although not, to be sure, in the eyes of her own theologians—and Prague's destiny could hardly be different. Charles's son, Wenceslas, succeeded his father both as emperor and as king of Bohemia, but in the early 1380s he began to turn away from imperial interests and from the whole universalistic tradition of his father. Without pursuing any sort of Bohemian ideal, he failed also to pursue any lofty aim at all, and thus his reign marked a turning point in the development of the Bohemian nation. The leading German ornaments of Prague's religious and cultural life left the realm, and the Czech element in Wenceslas's government grew.[17] That a comparable change began to take place at the university was probably due in part to the more or less incalculable effect of this shift on the consciousness of the Czech academics. What is more obvious is that it resulted from the natural process by which the succession of Czech students at the university had built up a corps first of Czech masters of arts and then of Czech masters of theology. The arrangements which reflected the older balance of nationalities could not survive these changes.

During most of the 1380s the inner life of the university was

[16] Friedrich von Bezold, "Die ältesten deutschen Universitäten in ihrem Verhältnis zum Staat," *Historische Zeitschrift* 80 (1898):436ff.; H. Rashdall, *The Universities of Europe in the Middle Ages*, ed. F. M. Powicke and A. B. Emden (Oxford, 1936), vol. 1, pp. 540ff.

[17] František M. Bartoš, *Čechy v době Husově 1378–1415* (Prague, 1947), pp. 42–44; I. Hlaváček, "Die Geschichte der Kanzlei König Wenzels IV," *Historica* 5:13f.

repeatedly disrupted by the struggles of Czech theology students —who were also professors in the Arts Faculty—to get places in the masters' colleges and by the opposition of the Czechs in the Arts Faculty to the efforts of the predominantly German professors of theology to secure a privileged status for their faculty.[18] We hear of a suspension of lectures by the Germans, of Czechs ignoring the suspension and coming to class under arms, and of actual fights, in one of which the rector, Conrad of Soltau, was wounded. The upshot was that, as the Czechs had no doubt foreseen, the King and the Archbishop imposed a settlement in their favor, giving them a definite share—about half—of the collegiate livings.[19] Soon after, in 1390, another conflict broke out over the issue of whether a master of German nationality belonging to the Bohemian nation of the university could profit from that nation's victory by receiving one of the livings allotted to it. Here too the Czechs won their cause, and henceforth, at least in matters of this sort, the Bohemian university nation belonged exclusively to Czechs.[20] In all of this the German masters took their stand on the rights and statutes of the university, on its original supra-national character, and on the fact of their vast numerical preponderance over the Czechs. But the latter could rely on other facts, chiefly the basic one, destined to become crucial, that they were the natives, the members of the Bohemian realm, while the Germans were foreigners. The resources of the masters' colleges came from Bohemian properties and should support members of the Bohemian nation. The King, the Archbishop, and most of the people of Prague could also be counted on to favor the Czech masters' cause, for either political or ethnic reasons. Not only the final decision but even the language used by the Archbishop's court represented the true situation: all the German foreigners were lumped together as the "*natio Teutunicorum*" in opposition to the Bohemian nation.[21] There were thus

---

[18] R. Weltsch, *Archbishop John of Jenstein* (The Hague, 1968), pp. 158–61; Bartoš, *Čechy*, pp. 64f.

[19] F. Matthaesius, "Der Auszug der deutschen Studenten aus Prag (1409)," *Mitteilungen des Vereins für Geschichte der Deutschen in Böhmen* 52 (1914):473–78.

[20] *Ibid.*, pp. 478–80.

[21] *Ibid.*, p. 481.

only two parties, and the Czechs automatically secured a parity that neither their numbers nor the university's statutes entitled them to have.

It is at this point that we can see the pattern of Hus's cause beginning to take shape. At its center was the struggle of an emerging native intelligentsia striving to establish itself in the political society of what was still a semicolonial territory and seeking to gain the power, prestige, and wealth that were available in the university. Jerome of Prague, who matriculated in 1395 or 1396, expressed this immediate concern in his speech of justification at the Council of Constance, in 1416: "In the University of Prague there were many Germans, in church prebends and in the colleges, to the point that the Czechs had nothing. Hence when a Czech was graduated in arts, if he had no other source of income he had to earn his livelihood by being a schoolmaster in some town or village. The Germans had complete control of the university, its benefices, its seal, and its symbols; [they had three nations] and whatever they would do they did, and the Czechs could do nothing."[22] We have seen that the Czech struggle against this situation necessarily transcended the academic framework and could in fact be successful only because of the ties of interest or sympathy that associated the Czech cause with the Bohemian polity. These objective relationships became part of the Czech masters' consciousness, and the passage of Jerome's speech quoted here was followed immediately by the statement that the same situation prevailed outside the university—the Germans had sixteen out of eighteen of the places in the Prague town council, and "the whole realm was governed by Germans, they had all the secular offices, and the Czech laity counted for nothing." John Hus, who became a student at the university in 1390, expressed the same national-political sentiment in its more positive form: "The Czechs in the realm of Bohemia, according to human laws, divine law, and natural instinct, should be first in the realm's offices, just like the French in France and the Germans in their lands."[23] At a level well below this one the Czech

[22] Mansi, ed., *Sacrorum conciliorum*, vol. 27, cols. 891f.
[23] Palacký, ed., *Documenta*, p. 177.

cause drew power from simple ethnic hatred nourished by resentment, and a number of anti-German literary works were produced by Czech university members in this period,[24] but the direction taken by the Czech movement was determined by positive conceptualizations of the sort just quoted. Their emotional correlate was not simply anti-Germanism but a kind of religious patriotism, a conviction that the Czech nation was not only in the right but was positively holy.

The substance of this conviction was formed by the association of the Czech university nation with religious reform. A strong movement of lay pietism had been cultivated among the people of Prague — and the Czech people above all — by popular preachers like Konrad Waldhauser and John Milič. In the enlightened atmosphere of Charles IV's Prague some eminent German academics had associated themselves with the ideals of this movement. But a few years of Wenceslas IV sufficed to change the atmosphere, and in the 1390s the eminent Germans left. Some, like Matthew of Cracow, went to the new University of Heidelberg, where they helped prepare West German opinion for the deposition of Wenceslas in 1400 and his replacement as emperor by the Elector Rupert, Heidelberg's prince.[25] Their place in Prague was taken by the Czech masters of arts and theology, who now had places in the colleges, increased access to university offices, and a habit of identification with the national cause. Their new substance also involved them more and more closely with the Czech burghers of Prague and with both Czech and German members of the royal court. Professors and burghers appeared together in civil actions, wealthy Praguers founded endowments for Czech academics,[26] and the Czech masters began to take an active interest in the Czech religious movement. When in 1391 a German member of the royal court and a prominent Czech citizen of Prague jointly founded Bethlehem Chapel

[24] See Šmahel, "The Idea of the 'Nation,'" *Historica* 16:162.

[25] For a brief list of the German reformers, see Seibt, "Die hussitische Revolution," p. 78; see also Weltsch, *Archbishop John of Jenstein*, passim. For the Heidelberg activity, see Bartoš, *Čechy*, pp. 179f.; *HHR*, p. 60.

[26] See, e.g., Otakar Odložilík, *M. Štěpán z Kolína* (Prague, 1924), p. 21.

in Prague's Old Town for preaching in Czech, they provided
that the preachers be nominated by the Czech theologians of
Charles College together with the burgomaster of the Old
Town.[27] Master Stephen of Kolín, one of the new group of successful Czech careerists, held the post from 1396 to 1402; his suc-
cessor was his pupil, John Hus. These institutional arrangements,
amplified by the founding of a students' college in connection
with the Chapel, not only secured the continuance of the popular
movement but allowed its themes of pietism and selfrighteousness
to resonate with the mentality generated by the Czechs' drive for
status in the university. The nation was becoming holy. In 1409,
when John Hus recalled to his audience the names of the leading
Czech masters of the older generation, it was precisely Master
Stephen of Kolín, the preacher of piety, whom he chose to
decorate with the epithet "most fervent of patriots."[28]

If the masters had not gone beyond this level of association
of academic, national, and religious strivings, there would have
been no Hussite revolution or reformation. The fatal step was the
move from an entirely pragmatic drive for power and status to
identification of their cause with a comprehensive theory that
conceptualized all of their aims in terms of a national ecclesiology, the doctrine of John Wyclif. The philosophy of Wyclif,
based on the belief that universals were real, had found acceptance among some Czechs from an early date, perhaps as early as
1380, and it served, among other things, to differentiate them
from the Germans, most of whom seemed to have held the oppo-

[27] Otakar Odložilík, "The Chapel of Bethlehem in Prague. Remarks on Its
Foundation Charter," *Studien zur älteren Geschichte Osteuropas*, vol. 1, ed. G.
Stökl (Graz and Cologne, 1956), pp. 125–41.

[28] *Iohannes Hus, Magister Universitatis Carolinae, Positiones, Recommendationes,
Sermones*, ed. Anežka Schmidtová (Prague, 1958), p. 126: "zelator patrie fer-
ventissimus." Neither Stephen's surviving works nor the pattern of his careerism
offer any clue as to why he deserved just this praise (see Odložilík, *M. Štěpán*,
p. 9; Šmahel, "The Idea of the 'Nation,' " *Historica* 16:166f.), and one guesses
that the reason was that his own drive to advancement necessarily involved a
struggle for the Czech academics' cause. At the same time his very career may
have been remembered by the younger, patriotic generation as a paradigm
of what they sought for themselves.

site philosophy of "nominalism."[29] But even a prominent Czech "realist" like Nicholas Biceps could combine his use of Wyclif's philosophy with a condemnation of the Englishman's religious doctrines,[30] and if the Czechs subsequently, around the turn of the century, took up the latter with enthusiasm, it was not merely because the doctrines were available. The Czechs were not the passive recipients of Wyclifism—they went out and got it. Jerome of Prague was only the most famous of a series of Czech scholars who went to England, copied the treatises in question, and brought them back home. We catch a glimpse of their ardor in a report of a letter that Jerome wrote from Paris after a trip to England, informing the older masters Stephen of Kolín and Stanislav of Znojmo of the books he had gotten for them and which they would be very happy to have.[31] But it is easier to ascertain this affinity than to account for it. Why should the Czech philosophers and theologians have taken up foreign doctrines which had already been condemned as erroneous or heretical and which could not fail to bring their movement into disrepute? Some of the Czech academics did indeed balk at Wyclifism for this reason; without ceasing to adhere to the national cause, including its component of pietist reform, they refused to follow their colleagues onto the new path.

[29] D. Trapp, "Clm. 27034. Unchristened Nominalism and Wycliffite Realism at Prague in 1381," *Recherches de théologie ancienne et médiévale* 24 (1957): 320–60, esp. pp. 354–56; F. Šmahel, " 'Doctor evangelicus super omnes evangelistas': Wyclif's Fortune in Hussite Bohemia," *Bulletin of the Institute of Historical Research* 43 (1970):16–34. Šmahel notes (pp. 18–20) that genuine espousal of Wyclif's metaphysics by the Czechs seems to date from the 1390s; any previous use of Wyclif's "extreme realism" was within the framework of the "moderate realism" of the first Czech academic philosophers. Whether or not realism (i.e., idealism) was more progressive, more apt to validate reform than nominalism (i.e., materialism) seems to me an artificial question, but it has gotten a lot of play. See R. Kalivoda, *Husitská ideologie* (Prague, 1961), pp. 87ff., for an argument in the affirmative; Šmahel, in "Doctor evangelicus" and in "The Idea of the 'Nation,' " *Historica* 16:164f., canvasses the pros and cons. Prague philosophy of this period urgently requires systematic study, based on the still unpublished sources.

[30] Trapp, "Clm. 27034," pp. 354–56; Evžen Stein, "Mistr Mikuláš Biceps," *Věstník Královské české společnosti nauk, třída filos.* no. 4 (1928), esp. pp. 13, 43f.

[31] R. R. Betts, "English and Czech Influences on the Hussite Movement," *Essays in Czech History* (London, 1969), pp. 132–59; Odložilík, *M. Štěpán*, p. 18.

Before offering an explanation, it will be useful to summarize the relevant aspects of Wyclif's ecclesiology.[32] It was based on the definition of the true church as the community of all predestined to salvation, past, present, and future; the true church in this world consisted of those predestined who were currently alive. On this basis Wyclif formulated his key position that no actual human institution could claim to be this community, for only God knew who was predestined. The Roman Church, including as it did all Christians, could therefore not claim the prerogatives of sanctity for its administrative system, its fiscalism, its judicial system, its legal privileges within the various realms, or the civil dominion that it held over property and people. The power, wealth, force, and coercive jurisdiction necessary to any human government, including the government of the Church, were signs of imperfection. They could not belong to the clergy, who had to follow the perfection of Jesus by obeying his evangelical law; they belonged rather to secular governments. Such governments were admittedly imperfect, but it was their divine mission to use power to enforce God's law in its wider sense. The product of this system was what Wyclif himself called "political religion"—each church was, as an institution, coextensive with its realm, and was to be governed by that realm's secular powers. Its fellowship with other churches, which Wyclif did not reject, could only be spiritual and voluntary, a communion of faith and doctrine; and this also applied to the fellowship of a territorial church with the Church of Rome. It will be evident that this political religion presupposed a good deal, especially the English reality of a well-developed polity, a strong Crown, and solidly established estates whose ties of rights and duty to the Crown had been worked out through generations of conflict and collaboration. In this sense Wyclifism can be characterized as a theoretical model of the regime of estates in its Christian aspect.

Its appeal to the Czech academics can now be understood. Educated to the level of the more advanced countries of the West, they formed their concepts of the possible and desirable in harmony with those cultivated in Paris and Oxford. Their ideal of

[32] For what follows see *HHR*, pp. 23–35.

their proper status required for its realization the sort of self-sufficient territorial polity, established on the basis of well-defined legal relationships linking Crown to estates, that existed in realms like England and France. But in Bohemia these relationships were underdeveloped. The baronial and noble estates had rights and institutions that rivaled those of the Crown; the important towns were royal property and had made only fragmentary progress in their effort to secure definite legal rights as an estate of the realm; the Church was caught between regular exploitation by the papacy and spasmodic plundering by the Crown.[33] Thinking of their destiny in terms of a Bohemian realm run by Czechs, the masters could formulate a program only by visualizing a transformation of reality; their political thought had to be theological, rather than, say, legal. Wyclifism, which was too rigorously abstract to find adequate response in England at this time, was thus ideally suited to such a cause.

It did, to be sure, have its disadvantages. It included a politically superfluous eucharistic deviation that laid some of its Czech adherents open to charges of error or heresy; but others, like John Hus, simply omitted to embrace that doctrine. Its ecclesiology had, as already noted, been condemned, and for good reason, for it was certainly subversive of the papal system. It is instructive that sooner or later every Czech who reached the top of the academic ladder, i.e., a professorship in the Theology Faculty, rejected Wyclifism. But many of the rest, including John Hus,

---

[33] Bartoš, Čechy, pp. 113ff.: "Power in the Bohemian state was divided between the king and the nobility. The former was lord only on royal ground—on crown estates, including the property of monasteries and of course the property of vassals—and in the towns. All else was in the hands and power of the nobility." That is, the nobility proper had not been feudalized under the Crown nor brought into the Western form of chartered relationship between estate and Crown. For the situation of the Church, see pp. 231ff.; cf. also Weltsch, Archbishop John of Jenstein, pp. 46f, and passim; Jaroslav Eršil, Správní a finanční vztahy avignonského papežství k českým zemím ve třetí čtvrtině 14. století (Prague, 1959), pp. 129ff. (a summary in French). On the inconclusive struggles of the towns for political status in the fourteenth century, see Ferdinand Seibt, "Der Zeit der Luxemburger und der hussitischen Revolution," in Handbuch der Geschichte der Böhmischen Länder, ed. K. Bosl, vol. 1 (Stuttgart, 1967), p. 426 and passim; also Frederick Heymann, "The Role of the Towns in the Bohemia of the Later Middle Ages," Journal of World History 2 (1954):326–46.

found in it so perfect a theory for validation of their aspirations that they could not conceive of giving it up, even when they might usefully have done so. In 1403 it was possible for the Germans at the university to strike back at the Czech movement by having the university condemn a list of forty-five of Wyclif's "articles," and from that time on the cause of the Czech masters was indistinguishable from Wyclifism. Nothing is more striking in this connection than the way in which the masters insisted on defending Wyclif's predestinarian definition of the Church in the years 1415–1417, when the key issues facing the Hussites were those of Utraquism and radical sectarianism, not the abstractions of academic theology.[34] To the masters, of course, these abstractions were formulations of the essence of their cause. And it may be remarked here that certain of the more workaday elements of Wyclifism, especially the doctrine of evangelical poverty for the clergy, were never subjects of the masters' enthusiasm. Wyclif himself had not insisted on real poverty, although he praised it as the best way. He prudently allowed for a system of transferring civil dominion over church property to the laity, with the clergy still enjoying the revenues, and this was what the Prague masters held, much to the disgust of the radicals.[35]

The full exploitation of Wyclifism's value as the political religion of the Czech cause came in 1408 and 1409, after the first generation of Wyclifite leaders gave way to the younger group led by John Hus. In May of 1408 Master Stanislav of Znojmo, the leader of the party, was ordered by Pope Gregory XII to appear at the papal court to answer to accusations of Wyclifite eucharistic heresy (a citation procured by the German masters acting in collaboration with the University of Heidelberg). Under this pressure a meeting of the Czech university nation, on 24 May, felt obliged to help its leader by condemning the list of forty-five Wyclifite articles whose condemnation by the university had been accomplished by the German majority five years

[34] Otakar Odložilík, "Z počátků husitství na Moravě. Šimon z Tišnova a Jan Vavřincův z Račic," Časopis matice moravské 49 (1925):1–170, esp. 53–78; Palacký, ed., Documenta, pp. 663–65.

[35] HHR, pp. 153, 202. On one occasion John Hus interpreted Wyclif's doctrine of civil dominion in terms of the king's right to tax the clergy (HHR, p. 94)—an instructive expression of the relationship between evangelical poverty and the Ständestaat.

earlier. At this low point John Hus took up the leadership that Stanislav had to abandon, and, working closely with Jerome of Prague and John Jesenic, he directed the Czech effort not along lines of doctrinal exploration but of political action. The opportunity was at hand. Pope Gregory's cardinals had withdrawn their obedience from him in order to try to end the Great Schism, and they summoned the rulers of Europe to do the same; in June they united with the Avignon cardinals in a call for a general council to meet at Pisa in March of 1409. French policy had long been directed toward this action, and a French embassy was sent to Wenceslas to persuade him to go along. The cardinals for their part held out the hope that his title of king of the Romans might be recognized by the new pope who would emerge from Pisa. But Archbishop Zbyněk of Prague refused to give up his obedience to Gregory, and when the issue was discussed at the University of Prague, the German masters also refused. Most of them came from lands that recognized Rupert as emperor; since he supported Gregory, they feared for their future careers if they were to support the cardinals. Furthermore, as we have seen, their struggle against the Czech Wyclifites had been developed in association with Rupert's University of Heidelberg. King Wenceslas naturally thought that his university should support *his* policy—such was, in fact, the function of a territorial university—and on this occasion he needed that support. The Czechs' hour had struck.

John Hus began to prepare his flock in Bethlehem for the events to come, even while he and Jerome increased their cultivation of the nobility and certain members of the royal court. At about this time too, or perhaps somewhat earlier, Hus and Jerome prevailed upon the King—we do not know how—to change the balance in the Prague town council to a Czech majority.[36] It would not be an overstatement to say that the particular and miscellaneous ties between the Czech masters and the

[36] In his last statements at Constance Jerome said that he and Hus had accomplished this and also referred to Hus's sermons urging his flock to support the Czech effort to end German domination (Mansi, ed., *Sacrorum conciliorum,* vol. 27, col. 892). Recent research confirms at least the result he claimed: Šmahel, in "The Idea of the 'Nation,' " *Historica* 16:173, and in his *Jeronỳm Pražský* (Prague, 1966), p. 81, cites the as yet unpublished work of J. Mezník to this effect.

elements of Bohemian society—insofar as the latter was focused in Prague and the royal court—were being drawn into a political structure under Hus's leadership. And it was as part of this enterprise that Hus kept the lines of communication open even with the anti-Wyclifite Czech masters, including the doctors of theology, who were willing to use the political crisis to establish Czech domination of the University. As for Wyclifism, it too benefited from the new situation, for the King could not effectively pursue any policy in the schism if his realm were suspect of heresy; he therefore prevented the archiepiscopal officials from pursuing their activity against the Wyclifite leaders.

If the Czech drive to gain control of the university came to a head in the circumstances of 1408–1409—and we shall return to them in a moment—it nevertheless drew its main force from long-term developments within the institution itself. Neither the Czech masters' victories of the 1380s nor the competition from the new universities in Germany had had more than a transitory effect on Prague's growth, whose rate of increase actually rose in the years 1399–1409. Not counting the enrollment at the separate Law University, there were more than a thousand students at any given time in this decade. But most of the increase came from abroad. While the number of Czech students also increased, they represented only about 20 percent of the total during the decade, and in the last two or three years this figure fell to 16.5 percent. Presumably the Czech masters were aware of this trend—not in the form of percentages but in a sense that the foreign element was getting stronger and stronger. At the same time, the Czechs certainly realized that their students were on the average better than the others; they placed higher in their examination even though each examining board was composed of masters from all four nations. [37] But the most important factor

---

[37] František Šmahel, *Pražské universitní studentstvo v předrevolučním období 1399–1419*, Rozpravy Československé Akademie Věd, Řada společenských věd, vol. 77 (Prague, 1967), p. iii, offers a statistical analysis of the student body during the period; pp. 16–37 discuss the size of enrollment. He includes many of his results in his "Le mouvement des étudiants à Prague dans les années 1408–1412," *Historica* 14 (1967):33–75; see esp. pp. 38, 42, 55, for the facts I have given above.

in the thinking of the Czech masters of arts must have been their sense of their own numerical force. Of the total number of regent masters—those carrying on regular teaching of the required curriculum and taking part regularly in the administrative and pedagogical functions of the faculty—the Czechs formed 16.6 percent in 1371–1380, 19.3 percent in 1381–1390, 26 percent in 1391–1400, and 29.3 percent in 1401–1409.[38] Furthermore, while most foreign masters would sooner or later leave Prague to pursue their careers back home, the Czechs naturally tended to stay around. In the period 1390–1409 there were 135 new foreign regent masters promoted, of whom 80 (about 60 percent) left after the required one or two years of teaching in Prague; of the 50 new Czech regent masters in this period, only 13 (26 percent) left after one or two years.[39] This difference, along with what was doubtless an even more pronounced one among the non-regent masters, accounts for the fact that, in the academic year 1408–1409, 12 of the 36 regent masters of arts were Czechs, while at the same time the total number of Czech masters of arts in Prague was much greater, probably equal to the total number of foreign masters; we know that in 1411 there were more than 60 Czech masters.[40]

The sense of these figures is clear enough. Partly through their own hard work, partly because of the circumstances of being natives of the region, the Czech intelligentsia had reached a point of quality and quantity that made the domination of Bohemia's university by foreigners seem unreasonable and—no doubt—infuriating. At the same time the foreigners also had a great share of the professorial livings, while there were enough

[38] I draw these figures from František Kavka's statistical study of the regent masters of arts, "Mistři-regenti na artistické fakultě pražské university v letech 1367–1420," Z českých dějin. Sborník prací in memoriam Prof. Dr. Václava Husy (Václav Husa Commemorative Essays)(Prague, 1966), pp. 77–95, esp. p. 84.

[39] My calculations from Kavka's tables, ibid., pp. 82f.

[40] Hus's quodlibetical manual of 1411 lists sixty-six masters, almost all Czechs (Magistri Iohannis Hus Quodlibet. Disputationis . . . a. 1411 habitae Enchiridion, ed. Bohumil Ryba [Prague, 1948], pp. 219f.). According to John Příbram's later testimony, in 1408 the Bohemian nation counted about sixty doctors and masters: (Konstantin Hofler, Geschichtschreiber der husitischen Bewegung in Böhmem, in Fontes rerum Austriacarum, vol. 6: Scriptores [Vienna, 1865], p. 138). Cf. Kavka, "Mistři-regenti," pp. 87–89.

Czechs to covet each of these. But with the percentage of foreign students constantly increasing (it eventually amounted to more than 80 percent), the Czechs had no reason to be optimistic. The rights that they should have had by merit, by equity, and by national privilege were set beyond their reach by the statutes of a half-century ago. It is no wonder that in 1408 Hus, Jerome, and Jesenic decided to seize the favorable political opportunity and press for the Bohemianization of the university.

The final act in their preparations came in the first week of January 1409 at the quodlibetical disputation scheduled to be conducted by the Czech master Matthew of Knín. [41] The *quodlibet* was the major academic event of the year: the master named to direct it had to prepare scholarly questions in all disciplines, assign each master a question, and prepare his own question and also the outlines of what he would say in disputing with each of the masters. [42] The whole ceremony lasted several days and constituted a major academic effort; the university statutes made attendance and participation compulsory, on pain of a heavy fine. But this year the Germans said they would boycott the exercise because Knín was suspected of Wyclifite heresy. At this point Jerome of Prague moved in. Procuring a royal decree which ordered the Germans to attend, he invited the French and Brabantine envoys in Prague to come as guests, and the councilors of Prague's Old Town as well—the latter were royal appointees and now, thanks to the earlier action by Jerome and Hus, predominantly Czech. Jerome's own *questio* was a defense of Wyclif's metaphysical realism, itself a significant action; but the main event came at the end of the whole disputation, when he made a speech pillorying the Germans who had been unwilling to attend, defending the sacrosanct Czech nation against imputations of

[41] *HHR*, pp. 61ff., where references to the sources and modern literature can be found. Jerome's speech (below) is printed in Höfler, *Geschichtschreiber*, pp. 112–28. It has been the subject of much discussion; see Seibt, *Hussitica*, pp. 79ff.; Šmahel, "The Idea of the 'Nation,'" *Historica* 16:173ff.

[42] On the nature of the late medieval *quodlibet* at Prague, see Jiří Kejř, "Struktura a průběh disputace de quolibet na pražské univerzitě," *Acta Universitatis Carolinae, Historia Universitatis Carolinae Pragensis* 1 (1960):17–45, with English summary on pp. 51ff. For Knín's *quodlibet*, see Kejř's article cited in the next note.

heresy, exalting the sacrosanct city of Prague, and admonishing the town councilors to defend the cause of the Czech university nation, the King's friend. He tied all these themes together with classical maxims about the supreme virtue of love for the father-land, for which it was sweet and fitting even to die. Wyclif was also defended ardently and recommended to the students for their study. Jerome's purpose was evidently to establish the lofty status of the Czech university nation as publicly as possible, in order to prepare the ground for the King's expected intervention.

On 18 January the King summoned proctors from each uni-versity nation to attend him at Kutná Hora, where they were asked to support a royal decision in favor of subtracting obedi-ence from Gregory XII and taking part in the Council of Pisa.[43] The Germans all refused, but the two Czechs, the anti-Wyclifite theologians Andrew of Brod and John Elias, agreed. The proctors were then dismissed. Later in the day the King's council decided for the plan which Jerome, Hus, and Jesenic had prepared and which was straightaway issued, as what has come to be called the Kutná Hora decree: henceforth in all university functions the Czechs were to have three votes, the three German nations to-gether—called simply the *"natio Teutonica"*—only one. Copies were sent by special messenger to the university and to John Hus, who at the moment lay seriously sick in his Prague apartment. He had the pleasure of showing the decree to Brod and Elias, who had come to see him, and he later recalled how delighted they were over what they themselves called the "liberation" of the Czechs.[44] Subsequently, when the Germans tried to get the decree revoked and even agreed to send representatives to Pisa, King Wenceslas backtracked and promised them to restore the *status quo ante*. Hus and Jerome had to work hard to prevent him from doing so. We catch glimpses of them in these weeks, riding in a wagon to and from the royal court, and once even being threatened by the King with death by fire if they kept on making

[43] I follow the reconstruction by Kejř, "Sporné otázky v bádání o dekretu kutnohorském," *ibid.*, 3 (1962):83–119, with English summary on pp. 120f. For Jesenic's role, see Kejř, *Husitský právník, M. Jan z Jesenice* (Prague, 1965), pp. 12–23.
[44] Palacký, ed., *Documenta*, p. 181.

trouble. We also hear of how they kept the less resolute Czech masters in line by threatening to denounce them as traitors.[45] In the end they were successful, and on 9 May the royal councilor Nicholas Bohatý, together with the Prague town councilors, took the insignia of the university away from the German rector and dean and installed Czechs in their place. The Germans had previously compacted, masters and students together, that they would leave Prague if the royal decree were enforced. In the course of May they departed. At the end of June the King appointed Czechs to the vacated posts in the masters' colleges and the other university prebends that the Germans had held.[46]

The complex of ideas animating the Czech masters in their struggle found expression not only in Jerome of Prague's speech at the *quodlibet* but also in texts connected with the Kutná Hora decree. The decree itself justified the King's action by emphasizing the special status of the Czech academics as inhabitants of the realm, as possessors therefore of rights that the German foreigners did not have, and as members of the polity joined to their king by a common destiny. The university was clearly no longer regarded as an extraterritorial entity but as an integral member of the body politic, a basic conception no doubt reflecting the convictions of the Czech leaders, who must have been responsible for the text of the decree.[47] Later, during the temporary setback in the fight to keep the decree in force, John Jesenic wrote a defense of it, probably destined for Nicholas Bohatý and other patrons of the Czech cause in the royal council.[48] Here one sees best of all the peculiarly Wyclifite combination of national, political, and religious themes characteristic of the university movement under Hus's leadership. The law of the land was assimilated to the law of God; both gave the King the right to regulate the university in favor of the Czechs. Just as God had promised to make his people Israel supreme, so King Wenceslas was to make his people, the Czechs, supreme over foreigners in their own land. More practi-

[45] *Loc. cit.* Hus's reply was, "I never called any master a traitor."

[46] Bartoš, *Čechy*, pp. 309–12.

[47] The text of the decree in Palacký, ed., *Documenta*, pp. 347f. On its origins see Kejř, "Sporné otázky," pp. 95f.; Seibt, *Hussitica*, pp. 72ff.

[48] Palacký, ed., *Documenta*, pp. 355–63; *HHR*, pp. 67–69.

cally, the purpose of the university was to train men for public service; these should be Czechs, for "first and foremost in the councils of the king should be the sons of the kingdom, who have a native inclination to seek the kingdom's welfare—but this is not the case with foreigners." How unjust it was, then, that the Germans should have almost all the power, benefices, and professorships merely because once upon a time their numbers and superiority had entitled them to this status: "For now, with God's help, the fullness of time has come, in which the Czech masters have become more numerous than the Germans, and have been elevated above the foreigners in every science and faculty." It was right for the King to correct this inequity, and it was wrong for the Germans to protest that the university's privileges were above a royal decree: the King had every right to grant special privileges to inhabitants of the realm and to make law by new decrees as well as by authoritative interpretation of old ones. It was in fact the original sense of Charles IV's foundation that it would serve the native population above all. Subsequently, in another work, Jesenic drew the Wyclifite theme into the matter by identifying the Germans who were defaming the King and the realm from abroad as the very ones who had been defaming the Czech academics as Wyclifites. [49]

The masters now had everything they had been seeking for over a decade. If the religious component of their movement continued to develop, drawing in ever wider circles of the population and passing into reformation and revolution, all this was not because of the masters but in spite of them. They themselves had made no effort to involve any but the leading circles of the court and society; only a few of them—Hus, Jerome, Jesenic, Jakoubek —engaged in literary activity to widen the movement's base among the clergy and students. Even as professors they were rather inactive; few of them—again excepting Hus—maintained even an average level of pedagogic activity or of participation in the administrative functions of the university. [50] Only Hus, Jakoubek, and Jerome had much influence on the Czech stu-

[49] HHR, pp. 69f.
[50] Šmahel, "Le mouvement des étudiants," pp. 47–49.

dents, whose noninvolvement in the masters' movement up to 1409 probably suited the latter well enough.[51] Even the national ideals of the masters seem to have failed to evoke much of an echo outside their own ranks and those of the Czech nobility. Jerome of Prague's enthusiasm for the Slavonic rites of the Russians, his striking claim that the Czechs were descended from the Greeks, who had always been enemies of the Germans,[52] the Praguers' repetition, for propaganda purposes in 1420, of the story of how the Germans had destroyed the nationality of the Polabian Slavs a century or more before[53]—none of these manifestations of erudite ethnic pride resonated with the interests of the lower clergy or the common people. When the radical students went out to work with these groups, they found a Waldensian type of sectarianism far more relevant to the attitudes of the people—a sectarianism that rejected academic learning as at best a "waste of time."[54] In 1419 the people sang: "You who become masters with false learning, have you studied so that you could get wealth by clever flattery? You dress in silks, laugh at the Law of God, and wallow in pleasures!"[55] Everything that had made the masters' cause historically momentous is here disregarded as irrelevant; what is left is a bare imputation of motives that strikes very close to the bull's-eye.

If the core of masters remained loyal to Hussitism in spite of everything, it was because they could not salvage their cause

[51] *Ibid.*, pp. 46ff.

[52] Mansi, ed., *Sacrorum conciliorum*, vol. 27, cols. 846, 858, 891; for an English translation of the last passage see R. Watkins, "The Death of Jerome of Prague," *Speculum* 42 (1967):124–28. Seibt (*Hussitica*, pp. 82f) traces the medieval identifications, including putative descent, of Czechs and Greeks, Germans and Romans. I would throw in the guess that Jerome may have been thinking of a *Teucri-Teutonici* etymology.

[53] *HHR*, p. 369.

[54] *Articuli Valdensium*, edited most conveniently in J. Döllinger, *Beiträge zur Sektengeschichte des Mittelalters*, vol. 2: *Dokumente vornehmlich zur Geschichte der Valdesier und Katharer* (Munich, 1890), p. 339: "Item universitates scholarum Parysyensem, Pragensem, Wyenensem reputant esse vanam truffam et temporis perdicionem." For the Taborite expression of the same attitude, see Laurence of Březová's "Hussite Chronicle" in Jaroslav Goll, ed., *Fontes rerum Bohemicarum*, vol. 5 (Prague, 1893), p. 413: "Ad quid sunt nobis mistrzi fistrzi [evidently a play on the German *"Pfistermeister"*], cum in sola humana sapiencia dies suos confusive consumunt."

[55] *HHR*, p. 274.

otherwise. Both Czech and German anti-Wyclifites kept up a steady agitation designed to prevent the victory of 1409 from becoming permanent. The masters had no choice but to work for European acceptance of at least the principle of the reformation in which their own victory had been encapsulated. That meant a relentless struggle against the radicals and a correspondingly stubborn effort to get a king—Sigismund or a member of the Polish dynasty—who could guarantee the estate of everyone in the realm and lead it back into the European community. Pursuing these policies in 1419–1420, the masters were inevitably denounced by the Taborites as false prophets, satraps of Antichrist. By the middle of 1420 both the Taborites and their Prague ally John Želivský had come to see that the authority of the masters had to be destroyed: one of their demands of 5 August 1420 was that "the university masters be regularly subject to divine law, like other faithful Christians, and that they compose their writings according to the will of God, and deposit them in the Town Hall, so that they may be examined according to God's Law."[56] In November of 1421 Želivský's party demanded that "the masters deposit their own privileges, those of the university's foundation, and the university's statutes, in the Town Hall, so that it might be determined . . . if there was anything in them contrary to the Law of God." The determination would be made by Želivský's men, who would "strike out what ought to be struck and correct what ought to be corrected."[57] One thinks of the French royal government's attack on the privileges of the University of Paris—in a very different context, but to the same end, that of subjecting the university to ordinary control by secular power. Needless to say, the masters and their allies found ways of defending themselves and even counterattacking in a struggle that went on for decades. Želivský was murdered in 1422, Tabor was defeated at the Battle of Lipany in 1434, and soon after that the conservative Hussites got what they had been fighting for: the compacts of Basel allowed Hussitism to exist within the Roman church, and Emperor Sigismund was finally received as the

[56] Březová, "Hussite Chronicle," p. 398.
[57] Ibid., p. 531.

legitimate king of Bohemia. By this time, as we have seen, the university was only a ghost of its old self, but "the masters" were still on hand, their ranks thinned by death and weakened by age. As far as the present study is concerned, the epitaph of the story can be taken from a remark by Gilles Charlier, one of the Council of Basel's envoys to Bohemia: "The next day there came to us those who regard themselves as the University of Prague; among them was a certain old master Christian [of Prachatice] whom they called the rector of the university."[58]

[58] Quoted by Jiří Kejř, "Deklarace pražské university z 10. března 1417 o přijímání pod obojí a její historické pozadí," *Sborník historický* 8 (1961):154.

4 | The Radical Critics of Oxford and Cambridge in the 1650s

In the seventeeth-century English Revolution fundamental questions were asked about most existing institutions, including the universities. Criticism of Oxford and Cambridge at this period are normally discussed in the context of the history of science. English universities were notoriously backward in mathematics and science. Seth Ward, John Wallis, John Pell, John Milton, all left the universities and went elsewhere to acquire "the superstitious algebra and that black art of geometry."[1] The same was true of astronomy and medicine: "one had as good send a man to Oxford to learn shoe-making as practising physic," declared the great doctor Thomas Sydenham, who fortunately himself lacked a university education. The important scientific and mathematical work associated with the names of John Dee, William Gilbert, Thomas Hariot, Jeremiah Horrox, William Oughtred, John Wallis, and William Harvey went on outside the universities.[2]

From Bacon onwards the universities were under attack; the criticisms rose to a crescendo during the Revolution. John Hall in 1649, Noah Biggs in 1651, John Webster in 1654—their strictures

---

[1] Pell to Sir Charles Cavendish, quoted by Phyllis Allen in "Science in English Universities of the Seventeenth Century," *Journal of the History of Ideas* 10:229–38. Cf. Francis Osborn's ironical reference to "the black art of mathematics" and Thomas Hobbes on geometry as an "art diabolical" (see my *Intellectual Origins of the English Revolution* [Oxford, 1965], p. 55).

[2] K. Dewhurst, *Dr. Thomas Sydenham (1628–1689)* (Oxford, 1966), p. 17; cf. my *Intellectual Origins*, chap. 2, esp. pp. 53, 64, 303–4.

and demands are quoted by all historians of science and of the universities. There was a breakthrough in the 1650s, when a group of scientists gathered at Oxford, and for a brief period science seemed to have got a foot in the door, though the activities of these individuals received little or no encouragement from university officialdom. A critic like John Webster thought that nothing significant had changed; he was answered reassuringly, if tendentiously, by Ward and Wilkins, moderate reformers who were embarrassed by Webster's maximum program.[3]

If Oxford and Cambridge had been institutions whose main concern was to serve the secular and economic needs of society, the demands of the modernizers would have been irresistable. But they were not. The main function of the universities was generally agreed to be the production of parsons. From the sixteenth century on gentlemen in increasing numbers were spending a year or two at the universities but they usually left without taking a degree. Some might have dilettante scientific interests, though even Seth Ward thought this would not extend to dirtying their hands with chemical experiments.[4] In any case, their interests and needs were peripheral to the main function of the universities. Thomas Hobbes stated flatly that "the universities are the fountains of the civil and moral doctrine, from whence the preachers and the gentry . . . sprinkle the same upon the people"; "the instruction of the people dependeth wholly on the right teaching of youth in the universities"; "a university is an excellent servant to the clergy."[5] Hobbes's antagonist Bishop Bramhall agreed, observing that the attack on the universities was part of an attack on the clergy.[6] It is controversies over this function of the universities that I wish to discuss.

With the post-Reformation emphasis on preaching as the clergy's principal task, their education became of special impor-

---

[3] J. Webster, *Academiarum examen* (London, 1654); [J. Wilkins and S. Ward], *Vindiciae academiarum* (Oxford, 1654).

[4] See my *Intellectual Origins*, pp. 301–2.

[5] *Leviathan*, ed. C. B. Macpherson (Baltimore, 1969), pp. 728, 384; *Behemoth*, in *English Works*, ed. Sir W. Molesworth (London, 1842–45); 6:347; cf. pp. 184–85, 215–20, 230–34, 276–82.

[6] J. Bramhall, *Works* (Oxford, 1842–45), 3:478.

tance. The state church was a vast opinion-forming machine, comparable to the press, radio, and television today. During the century between Reformation and Revolution, church and universities had been reduced to dependence on the Crown. Oxford and Cambridge ceased to be effective self-governing corporations in the medieval sense. The colleges replaced the universities as the main centers of teaching, and the rule of the resident masters of arts was replaced by an oligarchy of heads of colleges. Direct government pressure influenced academic policy and appointments. Seventeenth-century university reformers wanted to reintroduce greater self-government into Oxford and Cambridge. Puritans criticized the type of clergy produced by the universities before 1640, the inculcation of Laudian, authoritarian ideas.[7] So, inevitably, the meeting of the Long Parliament in 1640 seemed to herald change. As early as December 1640 the House of Commons set up a committee to consider abuses in the universities. A year later the House found it necessary to deny "that we intend to destroy or discourage learning; . . . it is our chiefest care and desire to advance it." It announced that it did intend, however, "to reform and purge the foundations of learning, the two universities, that the streams flowing from thence may be clear and pure."[8]

During the civil war the universities as such took no significant part in national politics. Oxford was the king's military headquarters. Cambridge had royalist sympathies, but it had been reduced to submission by one of the earliest military exploits of Oliver Cromwell. Neither university was able to show any inde-

[7] George Kendall, *A Vindication of the Doctrine Commonly Received in the Reformed Churches* (London, 1653), Epistle and p. 3; cf. J. Trapp, *A Commentary on the New Testament* (Evansville, Ind., 1958; first published 1647), p. 460: "bemisted with the fog of superstition." For the stultifying effect of the enforced conformity of the 1630s, see, for example, Joseph Mede, *Works* (London, 1672), pp. 865–66.

[8] "The Grand Remonstrance," in *Constitutional Documents of the Puritan Revolution, 1625–60*, ed. S. R. Gardiner (Oxford, 1906), pp. 229–30. In April 1645 *Mercurius Politicus* noted of an ordinance about Cambridge that it confuted royalist slanders that Parliament was opposed to learning (No. 79, pp. 723–24). Cf. Henry Burton, *Englands Bondage and Hope of Deliverance* (London, 1641), p. 29, quoted by J. F. Wilson, *Pulpit in Parliament* (Princeton, N. J., 1969), pp. 49–50.

pendent political initiative. From 1604 on Oxford and Cambridge were each represented in Parliament by two members, normally selected in practice by heads of colleges. In the Long Parliament John Selden (Oxford) and Nathaniel Bacon (Cambridge) were active until 1648, but after Pride's Purge in December of that year they slipped into the background.[9] During the period in which university reform was most actively discussed, Oxford and Cambridge were in effect unrepresented in Parliament.

After Parliament's victory in the civil war, purges of the universities to subordinate them to the new rulers of the state naturally followed. Some radical supporters of Parliament had seen a more fundamental link between universities and royalism. Thus the Leveller William Walwyn asked in 1644 "whether the party who are now in arms to make us slaves consists not chiefly of such as have had esteem for the most learned arts men in the kingdom?"[10] "Who are our jailers?" asked Nicholas Culpeper. "I say scholars."[11]

But these were extremist positions. Most members of Parliament, most Presbyterian and Independent divines, accepted the existence of a state church: they simply wanted to put it under new management. This was true even of a militant Independent like Hugh Peter, who proposed that half the colleges of Cambridge should be set aside for the sole purpose of training ministers,[12] or of a Fifth Monarchist like John Spittlehouse, who wanted colleges to teach foreign languages to students, who would then become missionaries.[13] With the collapse of episcopacy and Church courts at the very beginning of the Revolution, however, the problem suddenly ceased to be merely one of controlling the

[9] M. B. Rex, *University Representation in England, 1604–1690* (London, 1954), pp. 58–60, chaps. 6 and 8, passim.

[10] [W. Walwyn], The Compassionate Samaritane (1644), in *Tracts on Liberty in the Puritan Revolution, 1638–47*, ed. W. Haller (New York, 1934), 3:82.

[11] N. Culpeper, *A Directory for Mid-wives* (London, 1651), Epistle to the Reader.

[12] H. Peter, *A Word for the Armie* (London, 1647); *Good Work for a Good Magistrate* (London, 1651).

[13] B. S. Capp, "Extreme Millenarianism," in *Puritans, the Millennium and the Future of Israel*, ed. Peter Toon (Cambridge, 1970), pp. 86–87.

state church and became the maintenance of any effective establishment at all. In this new freedom religious sects sprang up everywhere, especially in towns, rejecting any national disciplinary organization. They stressed the autonomy of each congregation and elected their own ministers, who were often not ordained clergymen at all but "mechanick preachers," laymen of the middle and lower classes.[14]

> For human arts and sciences,
> Because you dote on them,
> Therefore the Lord will others teach
> Whom you count but laymen.

So sang the prophetess Anna Trapnel.[15] Such preachers either earned their living by laboring six days a week or were maintained by voluntary offerings from their congregations. They had no use for, and rejected on principle, the tithes which went to maintain the parish clergy.

Tithes, the compulsory payment of 10 percent of each man's earnings to a parson in whose appointment he normally had no say, had long been under attack by religious radicals. A survival from a predominantly agricultural society, they were especially difficult to collect in towns; they led to unedifying quarrels and bore especially heavily on smaller men in the countryside.[16] Many Puritans anxious to retain a national clergy would have preferred some less contentious form of maintenance—a stipend paid by the state, for instance. But short of this, there was general agreement that tithes and a national church stood or fell together. To suggest, as sectaries did, that all ministers should depend on voluntary contributions was tantamount to suggesting that most ministers should starve. One might be in favor of this or against it, but all agreed that this was the case.[17]

---

[14] See W. Y. Tindall, *John Bunyan, Mechanick Preacher* (New York, 1964), passim.

[15] *The Cry of a Stone, or a Relation of Something Spoken in Whitehall by Anna Trapnel* (London, 1654), pp. 42–43.

[16] See my *Economic Problems of the Church* (Oxford, 1956), chap. 5.

[17] M. James, "The Political Importance of the Tithes Controversy in the English Revolution, 1640–60," *History* 26:1–18.

So the "mechanick preachers" presented a double threat to the state church. On the one hand, unordained ministers, who had been to no university, would lack the training, the indoctrination, which ensured that quarrels among the clergy, however bitter, never called in question the existence of a national church. On the other hand, if tithes ceased to be paid, there would be no jobs for graduates to go to; there would be no uniformly trained ministry capable of receiving instructions from above, to act as a relatively united opinion-forming body. There would be no central control over the thoughts of the masses of the population. The heresies which proliferated in the 1640s—again, especially in urban centers—convinced conservatives that such control was absolutely necessary. A state church, universities, and tithes must all be preserved. "No universities, no ministry" was the theme of Presbyterian Thomas Hall and others: no learning, no confutation of heresy.[18] In the preceding chapter Professor Kaminsky showed how the emergence of Taborite revolutionary theories drove most of the reformist Prague masters back to a defensive conservative position.[19] Something very similar happened to Presbyterians in England in the 1640s.

Moreover, an important part of the revenues of both universities and their constituent colleges consisted of impropriated tithes—tithes which had been paid to monasteries before their dissolution at the Reformation, and which were now often received by laymen or institutions performing no pastoral functions. When James I at the beginning of his reign promised to restore royal impropriations to the Church and urged universities to do the same, he was lectured by the bishops, who convinced him that such misguided zeal would be fatal to the financial stability of the universities. Then too, impropriated tithes formed a significant part of the income of many gentlemen, not to mention the fear often expressed in the 1640s that those who refuse to pay tithes today will refuse to pay rent tomorrow.

[18] T. Hall, *The Pulpit Guarded with XX Arguments* (London, 1651), Epistle and p. 22; *An Apologie for the Ministry and its Maintenance* (London, 1660), pp. 56–57; R. B[oreman], *The Triumph of Learning over Ignorance* (1653), in *Harleian Miscellany* (London, 1744–46), 1:494–95.

[19] See pp. 79–81, 105 above.

Property interests linked the state church, universities, and a section of the ruling class. About 1654 Francis Osborn referred sardonically to a man who was "an impropriator, and so will be true to the priests' interest."[20]

The link was recognized by conservative contemporaries. Any treatise of the time which starts as a defense of learning is certain soon to get round to defending tithes.[21] "When they commend learning," observed Walwyn, "it is not for learning's sake, but their own; her esteem gets them their livings and preferments, and therefore she is to be kept up, or their trade will go down."[22] Earlier clerics had defended pluralism as necessary to learning.[23] Now not only plural claims to tithes but tithes themselves came under attack. Milton thought the abolition of tithes essential to liberty of conscience.[24]

I must define the word "radical." Here I use it to describe those who rejected any state church, both separatist sectaries, who opposed a national church on religious principles, and others—Levellers, Diggers, Fifth Monarchists, Ranters, etc.— whose opposition was part of a more general political, social, and economic program. I distinguish them from the more conservative supporters of Parliament, whether Episcopalians, Erastians, Presbyterians, or Independents, who approved in principle of a state church, and from those Baptists who were prepare to accept it in practice.

For the radicals, a state church, tithes, and the universities seemed to go together. They did not want to destroy the universities: they wanted to change their function, to secularize them, to end their role as factories for divines, who by academic training and source of income were inevitably bound to the status quo.

[20] F. Osborn, Letters . . . To Colonel William Draper, p. 7, in Miscellaneous Works (London, 1722), vol. 2.
[21] Anon., A Vindication of Learning From unjust Aspersions (London, 1646), pp. 1–2, 29; R. B[oreman], The Country-Mans Catechisme: Or, the Churches Plea for Tithes (London, 1652), pp. 3–4; The Triumph of Learning over Ignorance, p. 499; Edward Waterhouse, An Humble Apologie for Learning and Learned Men (London, 1653), esp. pp. 91–110.
[22] [Walwyn], The Compassionate Samaritane, pp. 37–38, in Haller, ed., Tracts on Liberty, 3:83.
[23] See my Economic Problems of the Church, chap. 10.
[24] J. Milton, Works (New York, 1931–40), 6:65, 101–5.

Introducing more science into the universities was very much a secondary consideration for such reformers. But once the universities had been secularized and existed to serve the commonwealth rather than the state church, then the utilitarian arguments of the scientific reformers were acceptable to anticlerical revolutionaries, many of whom wanted to expand the number of universities once they had been reformed and to increase the number of scholarships.[25] The separatist William Hartley explained in 1651 that he and his like wanted the universities well regulated, not abolished: "For human arts, who esteemeth them more than those termed separatists?" Human learning is good in its sphere, though it "in itself gives no more light than spectacles to a blind man."[26] Nor were the scientific reformers themselves disinterested in religion: one of them, Samuel Hartlib, denounced the universities' "show of upholding the name of learning, without any engagement towards the public concernments of the commonwealth of learning or of the church of God in the communion of saints."[27] There was a convergence.

For the radicals the crux was the universities' role as a fountain of ministers for the state church. The accusation of wishing to destroy learning[28] has deceived some historians, but it is no more true than that most student revolutionaries today want to destroy the universities. The enemy was the close if invisible link which bound the ideologists produced by the universities to the values of the society in which they functioned. Seventeenth-century radicals had a word for it: the universities were Antichristian.

This word calls for a moment's digression. Sixteenth-century Protestants inherited from medieval heretics the idea that the pope was Antichrist. This belief became almost the official doc-

[25] New universities were proposed for London, Durham, York, Bristol, Exeter, Norwich, Manchester, Shrewsbury, Ludlow, Cornwall, Wales, and the Isle of Man (see my *Intellectual Origins*, pp. 108–9, 124; R. L. Greaves, *The Puritan Revolution and Educational Thought*, [New Brunswick, N. J., 1969], pp. 55–56). For scholarships see *ibid.*, pp. 59–60.

[26] W. Hartley, *The Prerogative Priests Passing-Bell* (London, 1651), p. 6.

[27] C. Webster, *Samuel Hartlib and the Advancement of Learning* (Cambridge, 1970), p. 191.

[28] Cf. *Rump: Or an Exact Collection Of the Choycest Poems and Songs Relating to the Late Times* (London, 1662), 1:15: universities must be overthrown because they "maintain the language of the Beast."

trine of the reformed Church of England, taught by archbishops and bishops from Cranmer to Abbott, as well as by Puritans. Antichrist was associated especially with persecution of the godly, the use of political power in ecclesiastical matters: separatists came to regard bishops and the Church establishment as Antichristian. Other Puritans continued to hope for reformation, but ultimately they lost confidence, first in bishops, then in the king who supported them, finally in Parliament itself, which wished simply to replace a repressive Laudian church by a repressive Presbyterian church. Radicals came to think of any state church, and the ideology which went with it, as Antichristian. Gerrard Winstanley, the Digger, so described the class and property relations which the state church shared and justified. The Taborites, we recall, in 1419–20 had denounced the masters of Prague University as satraps of Antichrist, and Luther had similar thoughts about the academics of his day. We must bear such senses of "Antichristian" in mind when considering criticisms of the universities.[29]

The view that there should be no separate caste of ordained ministers, that divinity should not be taught in universities, *could* not properly be taught there—these views had a respectable Protestant ancestry. The Geneva Bible, the Bible most widely circulated before the Authorized Version, had a marginal note to Revelation 9:3 which equated doctors of divinity with locusts. The first edition of the Puritan *Admonition to Parliament* of 1572 attacked doctors, though this was prudently expunged in the second edition.[30] Separatists like Robert Browne, John Greenwood, and Henry Barrow thought universities "the very guard of Antichrist's throne."[31] Such views were repeated in the revolu-

---

[29] See pp. 105–6 above; J. M. Headley, *Luther's View of Church History* (New Haven, 1963), pp. 207–8. See W. Lamont, *Godly Rule: Politics and Religion 1603–1660* (New York, 1969), and my forthcoming *Antichrist in 17th Century England* (Oxford, 1971).

[30] H. Schulz, *Milton and Forbidden Knowledge* (New York, 1955), pp. 186–87.

[31] A. Peel and L. H. Carlson, eds., *Writings of Robert Harrison and Robert Browne* (New York, 1953), pp. 530–31; L. H. Carlson, ed., *Writings of John Greenwood* (London, 1962), 1:268–69; L. H. Carlson, ed., *Writings of Henry Barrow*, vol. 1: *1587–1590* (New York, 1962), pp. 344–53, 534–41, vol. 2: *1590–1591* (New York, 1966), pp. 191, 211–24.

tionary decades by heretics as diverse as Cobbler How (the un-
learned are to be preferred for the ministry before equally gifted
learned men);[32] Lord Brooke ("the ways of God's spirit are free,
and not tied to a university man");[33] Roger Williams (God's
people do not need "the university, lazy and monkish," nor its
"superstitious degrees and titles of divinity";[34] the Baptist Henry
Denne ("as soon find" a true minister of the gospel "in the university of Newgate");[35] the Levellers Richard Overton (whose
Mr. Persecution had been "of all the universities of Christendom")[36] and Edmund Chillenden (the spirit is bestowed "as soon
upon a cobbler, tinker, chimney sweeper, ploughman . . . as to
the greatest, learnedst doctor in the world");[37] John Milton ("a
fond error . . . to think that the university makes a minister of the
gospel");[38] the vegetarian Roger Crab ("the Whore's great eyes
. . . are Oxford and Cambridge");[39] Henry Stubbe, the enemy of
the Royal Society ("antichristian universities");[40] the Ranter
Richard Coppin ("schools of Antichrist");[41] the Fifth Monarchist John Canne ("a nursery . . . not of Christ's but of Aristotle's
and the state's ministry");[42] the Quakers Richard Farnsworth
("Antichrist's methodical way in his school"), George Fox ("the

[32] Samuel How, *The Sufficiency of the Spirit's Teaching*, 8th ed. (London,
1792), pp. 36, 40–41, 51.

[33] Brooke, *A Discourse Opening the Nature of that Episcopacie, which is exercised in
England* (1642), p. 106, in Haller, ed., *Tracts on Liberty*, 2:150. Brooke is
ostensibly stating the views of others.

[34] R. Williams, *The Bloudy Tenent of Persecution* (1644), Hanserd Knollys
Society (London, 1848), pp. 263–65; *The Hireling Ministry None of Christs*
(1652), in *The Complete Writings of Roger Williams*, ed. P. Miller, 7 vols. (New
York, 1963), 7:169–72.

[35] H. Denne, *Grace, Mercy and Peace* (1645), in E. B. Underhill, ed., *Records
of the Churches of Christ gathered at Fenstanton, Warboys, and Hexham, 1644–1720*,
Hanserd Knollys Society (London, 1854), p. 377.

[36] [R. Overton], *The Araignement of Mr. Persecution* (1645), p. 40, in Haller,
ed., *Tracts on Liberty*, 3:250; cf. p. 228.

[37] E. Chillenden, *Preaching without Ordination* (London, 1647), p. 6.

[38] Milton, *Works*, 6:93; cf. p. 96.

[39] Crab, *Dagons-Downfall* (London, 1657). For Crab see my *Puritanism and
Revolution: The English Revolution of the 17th Century* (New York, 1958), pp.
314–22.

[40] H. Stubbe, *A Light Shining out of Darkness* (London, 1659), pp. 145, 150;
cf. pp. 92–106, 109–10, 139–50, 161–63.

[41] R. Coppin, *Truths Testimony* (London, 1655), p. 16.

[42] J. Canne, *The Time of the End* (London, 1657), sig. A 4v–6v.

Whore set up your schools and colleges . . . whereby you are made ministers"), Samuel Fisher ("learned lieutenants of Antichrist"), and many others.[43]

The essence of this radical emphasis was that God's grace was given direct to his elect: their inner light needed no priestly mediators. This was not always the mere doctrine of individualist anarchism which it appears at first sight. The spirit's message was not self-validating. Its acceptability was confirmed (or rejected) by the congregation after discussion, and this congregation was likely to be composed of men and women similar in background, aspirations, and needs. There is an analogy between the saint "speaking experienced truths" to a critical and sophisticated audience and the scientist describing experiments which can be tested by other scientists.

The execution of Charles I in January 1649, followed by the proclamation of a republic and the abolition of the House of Lords, roused radical hopes. But they were dashed by the defeat and suppression of the Levellers in the months which succeeded and by the apparent determination of the rulers of the commonwealth to pursue a conservative course. In May 1649, fresh from suppressing a mutiny of Leveller regiments at Burford, Oliver Cromwell assured Oxford University that "no commonwealth could flourish without learning."[44] He had just been given an honorary doctorate by the university, which had for so long been the king's military headquarters. In the next year Parliament augmented the stipends of heads of colleges, the agents of government control over the universities—"those little living idols or monuments of monarchy," as a contemporary called them.[45] Gowns were indeed "laid aside" while the army was in power,[46]

---

[43] R. F[arnsworth], *Antichrists Man of War* (London, 1655), pp. 53, 55; G. Fox, *The Lambs Officer* (London, 1659), p. 3; S. Fisher, *The Testimony of Truth Exalted* (London, 1679), p. 298; cf. pp. 589–90; cf. G. Fox, *Journal* (London, 1902), 1:7,11,236–37, 386. Cf. Greaves, *The Puritan Revolution*, pp. 24, 122–23, 133–36.

[44] *Writings and Speeches of Oliver Cromwell*, ed. W. C. Abbott, 4 vols. in 6, vol. 2: *Commonwealth: 1649–1653* (Cambridge, Mass., 1939), 2:73.

[45] W. Sprigge, *A Modest Plea for an Equal Commonweath* (London, 1659), p. 45; cf. my *Intellectual Origins*, pp. 311–14.

[46] Stubbe, *A Light Shining out of Darkness*, pp. 206–7.

118   CHRISTOPHER HILL

and hair (which Archbishop Laud had kept closely cropped) luxuriated in Roundhead Oxford. But John Hall in 1649, John Dury in 1650, and Noah Biggs in 1651 saw no hope of fundamental reform from within the universities and called on Parliament to undertake the task.[47]

In 1653 the meeting of the nominated Barebone's Parliament raised hopes for radical reformation of the universities. Pamphlets calling for reform were published throughout 1653 and 1654.[48] Looking back, we may judge that all this smoke concealed an absence of flame. The political defeat of the radicals had made real reform impossible. But contemporaries were frightened. The Vice-Chancellor of Oxford referred to "reports everywhere spread abroad concerning the abolition and destruction of the Colleges," and there were many more such remarks.[49] The dissolution of the Barebone's Parliament in December 1653 made Oliver Cromwell the savior of conservative society. David Masson was quite right when he wrote, nearly a hundred years ago, that "the Protectorate had come into existence not only in a conservative interest generally, but . . . especially for the preservation of an established church and the universities."[50] Pam-

[47] J. Hall, *The Advancement of Learning* (London, 1649), Dedication to Parliament; T. Dury, "A Supplement to the Reformed School," pp. 6–7, 11–12, in *The Reformed Library-Keeper* (London, 1650); N. Biggs, *The Vanity of the Craft of Physick* (London, 1651), sig. B 3–3v, pp. 229–30.

[48] The Epistle Dedicatory to Webster's *Academiarum examen* is dated October 21, 1653; cf. his *The Saints Guardian* (London, 1654), where the Epistle is dated April 28, 1653. Cf. also Samuel Hartlib's *True and Ready Way to Learn the Latin Tongue* (London, 1654), written in 1653 and dedicated to Francis Rous, speaker of the Barebone's Parliament. Hartlib's *Some Proposals towards the Advancement of Learning,* written in 1653 but never published, presumably because of the dissolution of the Barebone's Parliament, is printed by C. Webster in *Samuel Hartlib and the Advancement of Learning* (Cambridge, 1970), pp. 166–92. See also John Nickolls, *Original Letters and Papers of State Addressed to Oliver Cromwell* (London, 1743), pp. 99–102, 129.

[49] J. Owen, *Works* (London, 1850–53), 10:493–94. Cf. T. Fuller, *Comfort in Calamity* (1654), in M. Fuller, *Pulpit Sparks* (London, 1886), p. 242; [anon.], *A True State of the Case of the Commonwealth* (London, 1654), p. 16; Kendall, *A Vindication,* p. 3; *Calendar of State Papers, Venetian, 1653–1654,* p. 160; Anthony Wood, *History and Antiquities of the University of Oxford,* ed. J. Gutch (Oxford, 1786–92), 2:657; Anthony Wood, *Life and Times,* vol. 1: *(1632–63),* ed. A. Clark (Oxford, 1891), pp. 292–96; L. M. Payne, "Sir Charles Scarborough's Harveian Oration, 1662," *Journal of the History of Medicine* 12:163.

[50] D. Masson, *Life of John Milton Narrated in Connection with the Political, Literary and Ecclesiastical History of His Time,* 7 vols. (London, 1877), 4:566–68.

phlets attacked and defended Webster and other would-be reformers of the universities in political terms, as no better than Levellers.[51]

In September 1656 the Lord Protector told his Parliament that "God hath for the ministry a very great seed in the youth in the universities." But to this support for a state church he added a recommendation, for the benefit of army radicals, that these undergraduates "instead of studying books study their own hearts."[52] Cromwell's brother-in-law, John Wilkins, defended the universities because of their role in training ministers. In December 1656 John Evelyn heard him preach against ignorant sacrilegious officers and soldiers who would have destroyed learning.[53] Clearly the danger was over.

Against this background I want now to look in rather more detail at the views of two of the most radical critics of the universities, William Dell and Gerrard Winstanley. William Dell, Fellow of Emmanuel College, Cambridge, became a chaplain in the New Model army. We know little about him except from his own writings.[54] He held political views not far removed from those of the Levellers. In 1646 he was in trouble with some well-to-do London citizens and with the House of Lords for preaching (to a preponderantly army congregation) that "the power is in you, the people; keep it, part not with it."[55] When invited to

---

[51] Hartley, *The Prerogative Priests Passing-Bell*, pp. 9–10; W. Sheppard, *The Peoples Priviledge and Duty Guarded Against the Pulpit Preachers Incroachment* (London, 1652), p. 1; Webster, *Academiarum examen*, sig. A 4v, B 1v; [Wilkins and Ward], *Vindiciae academiarum*, pp. 6, 23, 43, 48; T. Hall, *Vindiciae literarum* (London, 1654), pp. 198–99.

[52] Abbott, ed., *Writings and Speeches*, 4:273.

[53] *Vindiciae academiarum*, pp. 3–4; Evelyn, *Diary*, 10 December 1656; cf. Edward Leigh, *A Treatise of Religion and Learning* (London, 1656), pp. 65–67, 91–97; Edward Reynolds, *A Sermon Touching the Use of Humane Learning* (London, 1658); T. Blake, *Vindiciae foederis*, 2d ed. (London, 1658), pp. 173–78.

[54] See H. R. Trevor-Roper, "William, Dell," *English Historical Review* 62: 377-79.

[55] *Lords' Journals*, 8:401, 403, 418; W. Dell, "The Building, Beauty, Teaching and Establishment of the truly Christian and Spiritual Church," in *Several Sermons and Discourses of William Dell* (London, 1709), p. 68. The passage quoted is not in the printed text of the sermon: see [anon], *A Vindication of certaine Citizens* (London, 1646), pp. 6–9.

preach before the House of Commons in the same year he spoke up on behalf of the poor. He was the first clergyman invited to preach there whom the Commons refused to thank and whom it did not ask to print the sermon. When Dell did print it, the Commons called him before the House.[56] Dell was apparently a republican earlier than this was fashionable. If Venice and Holland could do without kings, he asked, why should not England? He carried the principle of tolerance so far as to allow the tinker John Bunyan to preach at his Bedfordshire living of Yelden.[57] Dell took it for granted that "every free society hath power to choose its own officers"; *a fortiori*, the Church, the freest society of all, had this power.[58] He was thus already a notorious radical when in May 1649 he was elected Master of Gonville and Caius College, Cambridge—the first married man to hold that position.

Some of his critics alleged that Dell was antagonistic to learning as such. To demonstrate that this is untrue, we have only to look at his half-dozen pages on "The Right Reformation of Learning, Schools and Universities" (1653). Here he advocated the creation of schools in all towns and villages throughout the nation, where godly men and sober and grave women should teach English and the Bible. In cities and larger towns Latin, Greek, and Hebrew should be taught. Universities should devote themselves to those liberal arts useful to human society—logic, arithmetic, geometry, and geography, and to medicine and law when these had been reformed from their corruptions and disorder "both for practice and fees."[59]

Dell's radical political assumptions underlie his approach to university reform. Now that England has become a commonwealth, he argued, and tyranny has been replaced by freedom, Oxford and Cambridge should lose their monopoly. Universities or colleges should be set up in every great city in the nation. The state should allow these colleges a competent maintenance for

---

[56] Dell, *Several Sermons*, p. 158; Wilson, *Pulpit in Parliament*, pp. 88, 92.
[57] A. G. Matthews, *Calamy Revised* (Oxford, 1934), pp. 161–62.
[58] Dell, *Several Sermons*, pp. 246, 251.
[59] *Ibid.*, pp. 642–48.

godly and learned men to teach languages and arts "under a due reformation." Undergraduates could thus live at home, and so money would not be needed for scholarships. They should work their way through the university, earning their living in some lawful calling part of each day, or every other day. In this way twenty times as many undergraduates could attend the universities. After graduating, such men could act as ministers while supporting themselves, and so an end could be put to state maintenance for ministers. If a congregation wished it might support a full-time minister by voluntary contributions, without, however, calling on the authority of the state: "This reformed use of tongues and arts justly hath its place in the world." Even if all men cannot be Christians, yet all can be "improved in the use of reason and sober learning, whereby they may be serviceable to the commonwealth." "Human learning hath its place and use among human things," though it "hath no place nor use in Christ's kingdom."[60]

"It is one of the grossest errors that ever reigned under Antichrist," Dell told his Cambridge congregation in 1651, "to affirm that universities are the fountain of the ministers of the gospel"[61] or that clergy should be a separate caste. Scholar or clergyman, gentleman or trader, "if Christ call him and pour forth his spirit on him, that and that only makes him a true minister." Philosophy, arts, and sciences are useless to ministers. The word of God "cannot be learned as human arts and sciences can . . . by the teaching of men, together with their own pains and endeavors, but only by the teaching of God and his spirit."[62]

"The word of Christ . . . brings troubles, tumults, stirs and uproars in the world." "The rich, wise, learned and honorable" cannot endure this, and look back longingly to episcopacy, when "all things were well and in good order." The devil too "would have all things quiet, that he might keep his possession." "The

[60] Ibid., pp. 403–4, 642–48.

[61] George Fox quoted this phrase with approval, but added "Happy would Dell have been if he had lived what he spoke" (The Great Mistery of the Great Whore Unfolded [London, 1659], p. 154).

[62] Dell, Several Sermons, pp. 388, 398, 402–3. Dell quoted Luther in support; cf. p. 273.

dull and drowsy divinity of synods and schools cannot be the true word of Christ," since the world accepts it. It is "honored with degrees and scarlet, and the professors and publishers of it are in credit with men and worldly powers, and receive from them riches, honor and quiet life." Christ, however, calls to *his* Church "not the great and honorable and wise and learned, but mean, plain and simple people, . . . base and despised"—"poor, plain husbandmen and tradesmen" rather than the "heads of universities and highest and stateliest of the clergy."[63] "There is nothing but equality in [God's] church." Free discussion among equals, Dell argued along Miltonic lines, helps to keep out error, which may easily be introduced, "when one man only speaks."[64]

Cambridge, Dell told his university congregation, opposed the truth of the Gospel, derided and scoffed at it, relying instead on heathens like Plato, Aristotle, Pythagoras; on the "cold, vain and antichristian divinity" of Aquinas and Scotus; and on "the secular arm and worldly power (whom you have seduced for many ages)." The word of Christ is "contrary to the philosophical divinity of the schools and university, and the common carnal religion of the nation," reproving and condemning them.[65]

Dell quoted Hus to the effect that "all the clergy must be quite taken away ere the church of Christ can have any true reformation."[66] The chief rulers and pillars of the Church, "the most eminent and in appearance most godly and holy and orthodox of the clergy, are above all others most grievously offended at Christ" now, as in his lifetime.[67] In 1653 Dell accused the clergy of aiming to restore Presbyterianism "if they can gain the secular arm to strengthen them thereunto (of which now they have greatest hopes)." They want the magistrate to enforce a single national creed, he said, devised by "these men who are in academical degrees and ecclesiastical orders," "not for the magis-

---

[63] *Ibid.*, pp. 390–92, 395–96, 467; cf. p. 375.
[64] *Ibid.*, pp. 273–77, 297–300, 397.
[65] *Ibid.*, pp. 407, 419.
[66] *Ibid.*, p. 368. Dell frequently cited Wyclif, Calvin, Tyndale, Latimer, and Ridley against universities, as well as Luther and Hus (*ibid.*, pp. 552–53, 573, 576–78, 582, 590–95, 600, 610–12, 619–22, 628–38).
[67] *Ibid.*, pp. 381–82.

trate's advantage but wholly for the clergy's." But matters of faith should be determined by "the congregation of the faithful, and not universities and assemblies of divines." False prophets are to be found among ordained ministers, especially among "men of great worth and reputation" who appear to be "more than ordinarily godly, religious, wise, holy, sober, devout" and who win to their side "the greatest and highest persons in the kingdoms and nations." "For Antichrist could not deceive the world with a company of foolish, weak, ignorant, profane, contemptible persons, but he always hath the greatest, wisest, holiest and most eminent in the visible church for him." Antichrist "chose his ministers only out of the universities." "The chief design of Antichrist is to seduce the elect, seeing he hath nobody else in all the world that dare oppose him or know how to do it but you."[68]

He who has not Christ dwelling in his heart, who speaks the words of his own reason, wisdom, and righteousness, or other men's, or school divinity,[69] is a false prophet, "though his knowledge and religion be never so high and glorious, and holy also in the opinion of the world." Such men are false prophets even if "they speak the word of the letter exactly, . . . according to the very original and curiosity of criticism." "The word of Christ without the mind of Christ . . . is the effectual operation of error, whereby all hypocrites and false Christians are deceived . . . without all hope of recovery." A Church which has the word without the spirit is Antichrist's Church.[70]

False prophets are appointed by men as a result of their own desire and seeking, "through academical degrees and ecclesiastical ordination." They "sprinkle their sermons with Hebrew, Greek, Latin." They "will live by the gospel and not by the labor of their hands in a lawful calling. . . . They run . . . from a lesser to a greater living, and where they may gain most of this world, there will they be sure to be. . . . They especially desire to

---

[68] *Ibid.*, pp. 246, 466–69, 481, 483–84; cf. pp. 477–79.

[69] Defined as "an unlawful mixing of philosophy with the outward letter of the word" (p. 489); "a dead word . . . out of the books and writings of men" (p. 640).

[70] *Ibid.*, pp. 487–93.

preach to rich men . . . and care not much to preach to the poor, plain, mean people." For the sake of wordly advantage, false prophets force themselves upon congregations. They want preaching to be monopolized by those whom the civil magistrate has licensed; all others must be forbidden to preach. True prophets are slandered and persecuted, but are ready to testify to the truth with their properties, liberties, and lives; false prophets regard only worldly profit and preferment; they accept whatever party shall prevail. They fight against Christ in the name of Christ's Church. The godly must separate from the ministry of such false prophets, whatever reputation for godliness and orthodoxy they may have in the eyes of the world. The Bible says nothing about the whole nation being a Church: "Whatsoever a state, an assembly or council shall say ought not to bind the saints further than the judgment of those saints shall lead them." [71]

The universities are still fundamentally popish, governed by the statutes of their popish founders. The same philosophy and school divinity are taught there as in the darkest times of popery. Symbols and ceremonies—hoods, caps, scarlet robes—are all as in popery. Despite the reform of the outward face of religion in England, the universities remain "the strongest holds which Antichrist hath had amongst us." Degrees in divinity are Antichristian. A Turk or an infidel could take one "with a little time and pains—and money." [72] The system corrupts even good men who get caught up in it, "as we by sad experience have seen. Many men of great seeming religion, famous for preaching and praying, and reputed pillars in the church, when they have come hither into the university . . . have been entangled and overcome with the spirit of the university and of Antichrist, for worldly honor and advantage sake." [73]

A university education is useless for a minister who lacks the spirit, superfluous for one who has it. "Are grammar, rhetoric, logic, ethics, metaphysics, mathematics, the weapons whereby

---

[71] *Ibid.*, pp. 495–513; cf. pp. 397, 615–16; the last sentence is attributed to Dell in *A Vindication of certain Citizens*, p. 9.
[72] *Ibid.*, pp. 550–55, 558–60, 574, 603–8, 615–18, 626, 641.
[73] *Ibid.*, pp. 516–18, 525–26.

we must defend the gospel?" Dell asked. "Must that word be secured by Aristotle which delivers all the elect from sin, death and hell for ever?" The very virtues of the clerical caste, university-educated men learned in philosophy and languages, prevent them from distinguishing between Christ and Antichrist. "They verily think they oppose and persecute Antichrist himself when they oppose and persecute the faithful people of God." Subjectively Christian, they are objectively Antichristian. Covetousness is the key. Carnal ministers have a numerous (and profitable) audience because they speak what is in the hearts of worldy people. That is the case for separation, for Disestablishment, for ending the training of ministers in "the antichristian fountain of the universities."[74]

Dell's theories naturally upset his fellow dons. A young man called Joseph Sedgwick, preaching in Cambridge in May 1653, asked, "Is the university stipend, as paid to a divine, antichristian maintenance? Then under what capacity do Mr. Dell and his associates enjoy their places in Cambridge? . . . With what conscience can any Christian knowingly take the wages of Antichrist? I do not understand much honesty in cheating the Man of Sin of his money."[75] Dell did not reply, though he (unlike Sedgwick) surrendered his living at the Restoration rather than conform—when Wilkins and Ward became bishops. "No man knows the grievousness and efficacy of tribulation, and the weakness and frailty of human nature," said Dell mildly, "but they who have had experience of both." But Dell approached Winstanley's more secular analysis when he suggested that the reason why "all divinity is wrapped up in human learning" was "to deter the common people from the study and enquiry after it" and to make them turn to "the clergy, who by their education have attained to that human learning which the plain people are destitute of. . . . Then must it sadly follow, that all who want human learning must needs also want divinity; and then how

[74] *Ibid.*, pp. 516, 525–31, 535–38, 544, 602–3, 617.
[75] J. Sedgwick, "Learnings Necessity to an able Minister of the Gospel," in *A Sermon Preached at St. Maries, in the University of Cambridge* (London, 1653), p. 39.

shall poor plain people, who live in lawful callings and have not the leisure to attain human learning, how shall they do to be saved? . . . The necks of the people of the world have never endured so grievous a yoke from any tyrants as from the doctrine and domination of the clergy"—and this not only over their bodies and temporal estates; the clergy have also destroyed the people to eternal death.[76]

"When God shall undertake to reform his church," Dell warned, "all this sort of learning shall be cast out again as dirt and dung, and the plain word of the gospel only shall prevail." On that day "the elect shall not stand on compliments, formalities and niceties, nor regard friendship nor enmity; but . . . shall break through all that can be said by the wisdom, policy, prudence and religion of men, and shall execute the righteous judgments of the Lord" on the universities.[77]

I now turn from the Master of Gonville and Caius to the humbler figure of Gerrard Winstanley. Winstanley must have had a grammar school education in his native Wigan, for he quotes Latin. He came south as a cloth merchant and was ruined during the civil war. In April 1649 he and a group of poor men established a collective farm on common land at St. George's Hill, just southwest of London. Winstanley published a series of pamphlets to justify this short-lived experiment. He saw ownership of land as the key to political power. He thought that in consequence of the King's defeat in the civil war the common and waste lands should be restored to the common people to cultivate. With greater precision than Dell, he depicted the established church and the universities as defenders of existing power and property relations.

"Those that are called preachers . . . seeks for knowledge abroad in universities, and buys it for money, and then delivers it out again for money, for £100 or £200 a year."[78] In an elaborate metaphor Winstanley depicted evil as "a mighty spreading

---

[76] Dell, *Several Sermons*, pp. 371, 585, 597–99, 638.
[77] *Ibid.*, pp. 575, 580, 613.
[78] G. H. Sabine, ed., *The Works of Gerrard Winstanley* (Ithaca, N. Y., 1941), pp. 213–14.

tree," covering the earth with its branches "to keep it in darkness and to hide the sun of righteousness from it. . . . The universities are the standing pools of stinking waters, that make those trees grow; the curse of ignorance, confusion and bondage spreads from hence all the nations over. The paying of tithes, the greatest sin of oppression, is upheld by them." The clergy "became hearsay-preachers of the gospel," not from any testimony of the light within, but from book-learning. Yet the Apostles were mechanics, "fishermen, shepherds, husbandmen and the carpenter's son," who themselves spoke "as the spirit gave them utterance, from an inward testimony. Yet now these learned scholars have got the writings of these inferior men of the world (so called), [they] do now slight, despise and trample them under feet, pressing upon the powers of the earth, to make laws to hold them under bondage, and that lay people, tradesmen and such as are not bred in schools, may have no liberty to speak or write of the spirit." "The upshot of all your universities and public preachers . . . is only to hinder Christ from rising, and to keep Jacob under." Church and state are in an antichristian conspiracy to keep the young brothers servants and slaves. Any who dare oppose the clergy "are like to be crushed in their estates by the power of corrupt magistrates."[79]

"The university learned ones . . . make themselves ministers as men teach birds to speak." "Under a covetous, proud black gown" they "would always be speaking words, but fall off when people begins to act their words." The Pharisees still strive to kill Christ. Pope-like, they silence all who disagree with them.[80] Unlike Dell, Winstanley thought that even the maintenance of ministers by the voluntary contributions of their congregations was simply a more ingenious and subtle way "to draw people under a new bondage, and to uphold the hearsay-preaching, that in time matters may be wheeled about again to advance the scholars and give them the supremacy in teaching."[81] After the Digger colony had been forcibly dispersed, Winstanley summa-

[79] *Ibid.*, pp. 237–42.
[80] *Ibid.*, pp. 474–76; cf. p. 463.
[81] *Ibid.*, pp. 239–40.

rized his views in *The Law of Freedom* (1652). In his utopia one day in seven was still to be set apart for rest from labor, for mutual fellowship, and for education. The minister, elected each year by his congregation (like a tutor in the English adult education system), had no ecclesiastical functions; his duty was to keep people informed of current events and to instruct them in the laws of the commonwealth, in history, and in science. The history was to be slanted to show the benefits of freedom and the evil of tyrant kings: the science was to cover "physic, surgery, astrology, astronomy, navigation, husbandry and such-like." Members of the congregation were encouraged to contribute to the discussions, provided they spoke from experience, not from book-learning or hearsay.

To the complaint that this was a very utilitarian ministry, lacking in spiritual values, Winstanley replied in famous words which link the magical tradition of the Paracelsans and neo-Platonists with modern science, as so many of his contemporaries among the scientists were doing:[82]

To know the secrets of nature is to know the works of God; and to know the works of God within the creation is to know God himself; for God dwells in every visible work or body.

And indeed if you would know spiritual things, it is to know how the spirit or power of wisdom and life, causing motion or growth, dwells within and governs both the several bodies of the stars and planets in the heavens above and the several bodies of the earth below; . . . for to reach God beyond the creation, or to know what he will be to a man after the man is dead, if any otherwise than to scatter him into his essences of fire, water, earth and air of which he is compounded, is a knowledge beyond the line or capacity of man to attain to while he lives in his compounded body.

And if a man should go to imagine what God is beyond the creation, or what he will be in a spiritual demonstration after a man is dead, he doth as the proverb saith, build castles in the air, or tells us of a world beyond the moon and beyond the sun, merely to blind the reason of man. . . . A studying imagination . . . is the cause of all evil and sorrows in the world. . . . [It] puts out the eyes of man's knowledge,

[82] Cf. P. M. Rattansi, "The Intellectual Origins of the Royal Society," *Notes and Records of the Royal Society of London* 23:129–43.

and tells him he must believe what others have writ or spoke, and must not trust to his own experience. [83]

University divinity is made

a cloak of policy by the subtle elder brother to cheat his simple younger brother of the freedoms of the earth . . . The subtle clergy do know that if they can but charm the people by this their divining doctrine, to look after riches, heaven and glory after they are dead, that then they shall easily be the inheritors of the earth, and have the deceived people to be their servants. . . . Divinity came in after Christ to darken his knowledge; and it is the language of . . . Antichrist, whereby the covetous, ambitious and serpentine spirit cozens the plain-hearted of his portions in the earth. [84] . . . The secrets of the creation have been locked up under the traditional, parrot-like speaking from the universities and colleges for scholars. [85]

Thus Winstanley, like Dell though on a broader canvas, depicts the universities as tied to the social order; the function of the divines they train is to deceive and silence the people. Before reform is possible, the clergy's "mouths must be stopped," though "not by the hands of tyrannical human power," as they have stopped the mouths of others. [86] Winstanley, like Dell, envisaged a future in which the whole educational system should be widely extended, democratized, laicized, and made more scientific. This would ensure that "one sort of children shall not be trained up only to book-learning and no other employment, called scholars," who "spend their time to find out policies to advance themselves to be lords and masters above their laboring brethren, . . . which occasions all the trouble in the world." [87] "The use of human learning in this reformed way" would dissolve the greatest errors of Antichrist, and lead to his fall. [88] But for Winstanley, more clearly than for Dell, this was part of a general social revolution.

Consideration of the fundamental criticisms of Oxford and Cambridge as "a fountain of ministers" may perhaps be of more

[83] Sabine, ed., *Works of Winstanley*, pp. 562–66.
[84] *Ibid.*, pp. 568–70.
[85] *Ibid.*, p. 271.
[86] *Ibid.*, p. 241.
[87] *Ibid.*, pp. 562–66, 576–78; cf. p. 593; Dell, *Sermons*, pp. 642–48.
[88] Dell, *Sermons*, p. 647; Sabine, ed., *Works of Winstanley*, p. 570.

help in understanding their role in seventeenth-century English society even than consideration of proposed modernizations of the curriculum. It may throw light backwards and forwards on their unexpressed social role, unexpressed because never challenged except during the revolutionary decades. The shrill cries which the defenders of the universities then emitted show how vital a nerve had been touched.

It would be superfluous to labor modern analogies. The universities of seventeeth-century England were linked, through their ownership of impropriated tithes, with the prevailing property system—and with what the radicals thought to be one of its least satisfactory aspects. Their function made them liable to government pressures, and their oligarchical structure facilitated such pressures. The churches today have lost the political power and monopoly position of the seventeenth-century Church of England, but universities still play a part in transmitting the traditional culture in training the ideologists and the ruling elite of the future. Inevitably they tend to justify the values of the existing society; individuals employed in them may well ask whether they have been as successful as Dell in avoiding becoming "entangled and overcome with the spirit of the universities and of Antichrist, for worldly honour and advantage sake."

Where the analogy is incomplete is in our lack of knowledge of what seventeenth-century undergraduates thought. They were, of course, much younger than today's students. They were either sons of landowners or scholarship boys from poorer families: the career prospects of the latter, who became gentlemen by graduating from the university, were virtually restricted to the Church. If ministers were to be gentlemen, to attain to livings "full of all outward necessaries,"[89] they could not afford to attack tithes. Nevertheless, the Revolution must have had some unsettling effect on them. Dell himself noted that the young, "as being most free from the forms of the former age, and from the doctrines and traditions of men," were most easily brought over to independ-

---

[89] J. Pope, *The Unveiling of Antichrist* (London, 1646), p. 14; How, *The Sufficiency of the Spirit's Teaching*, p. 51.

ency.[90] The Earl of Clarendon, looking back, sourly noted a loss of "reverence and respect" in all social relations; "parents had no manner of authority over their children, nor children any obedience or submission to their parents; but everyone did that which was good in his own eyes. This unnatural antipathy had its first rise from the beginning of the rebellion.[91] But there is a gap in our knowledge here, which it would be nice to be able to fill. All we know is that many junior M.A.'s of Oxford—of the same age as today's undergraduates—wanted more university democracy and reform of the curriculum.[92]

Universities were crucial to the ideology of seventeeth-century society. It was not only that they had a monopoly of opinion-forming, training the persuaders. They also embodied and justified fundamental assumptions of the society—that all Englishmen were members of the national church, that only gentlemen educated in the classics might preach, that an ordinary layman must, in Milton's words, "resign the whole warehouse of his religion" to "some factor."[93] They denied by implication the fundamental Protestant doctrine of the priesthood of all believers, or at least appeared to restrict its application to educated believers. They had to be overcome before a democratic society could emerge. In fighting against them Dell and Winstanley were working for a more truly human freedom than those who accused them of disruption. Those who defended learning and a civilized way of life also defended tithes and, by implication, privilege.

In the seventeenth-century Revolution the radical critics of the universities failed as completely as the political radicals: the two failures are, of course, connected. In 1660 even spare-time scientists like Ward and Wilkins, who had defended Oxford and Cambridge against their more radical critics, were ousted from

[90] Dell, *Several Sermons*, p. 79.

[91] Edward, Earl of Clarendon, *Life* (Oxford, 1759), 2:39.

[92] [Anon.], *Sundry Things from several Hands concerning the University of Oxford* (1659), in *Harleian Miscellany*, 6:80–84. Cf. Leyborne-Popham MSS. (Historical MSS Commission), pp. 4–5 (a petition to Parliament in 1642 from "divers" of Oxford).

[93] Milton, *Areopagitica* (1644), in *Complete Prose Works* (New Haven, 1953), 2:544.

the universities. The *ancien régime* came back to Oxford and Cambridge, if to nowhere else in the kingdom. Modern science had to develop, slowly, elsewhere: in the Royal Society of London, in the dissenting academies. The universities retained their monopoly of training parsons for the state church. The political significance of this changed when the Church lost its monopoly after 1689, but the universities were not reformed until the nineteenth-century.

This last chapter brings the study of universities in politics closer to the present day than any other in this volume, so it is not inappropriate to emphasize that Dell, Winstanley, and other radical critics were looking forward in the seventeenth century to the modern secular and scientific university as well as to the modern secular state.[94] We must not exaggerate their modernity; yet it is right to recognize the logic of events which made the radicals in the English Revolution adumbrate something of the modern world. The French Revolution expelled priests from the Sorbonne; Oxford and Cambridge were reformed in the nineteenth century, from outside, by Parliament, as seventeenth-century radicals knew they would have to be. Whether we have gone as far as Dell and Winstanley would have wished is another matter. The radicals attacked monopoly and professionalism, in medicine and law as well as in religion.[95] All three professions have now, I suppose, been thrown open to free market competition, though it is less evident that doctors, lawyers, and parsons are the servants of a democratic community in Winstanley's sense. Whether universities can be adapted to serve as a democratic community or are inextricably trapped in the power and property relations of our competitive society, as seventeenth-century Oxford and Cambridge were in their hierarchical society —these are questions currently under debate in most universities of the Western world.

[94] They have been treated much more sympathetically by American than by English historians: see Martha Ornstein, *The Role of Scientific Societies in the Seventeenth Century* (Chicago, 1928), p. 245; Greaves, *The Puritan Revolution*, p. 168.

[95] *Ibid.*, pp. 137–38, 146.

Notes on Contributors

Authors:

J. K. HYDE is Lecturer in Medieval History at Manchester University. Trained at Oxford University, he has specialized in the history of the Italian cities during the communal period. In addition to articles, he has published *Padua in the Age of Dante* (1966).

JACQUES VERGER is a member of the École Française de Rome. A graduate of the École Normale Supérieure at Paris, he also studied at the École des Hautes Études. He taught medieval history at the University of Tunisia before joining the French School at Rome. His interest in the late medieval university is revealed in a study, "Le Recruitment géographique des universités françaises au début du XVe siècle" in the *Mélanges d'archéologie et d'histoire* (1970).

HOWARD KAMINSKY is Professor of History at the University of Washington in Seattle. Educated at the University of Chicago, he has taught at Stanford University and the University of Wisconsin at Milwaukee as well as at the University of Washington. His scholarship in the late Middle Ages is best represented by his book *A History of the Hussite Revolution* (1967).

CHRISTOPHER HILL is Master of Balliol College at Oxford University. Educated at Balliol College, he has spent most of his academic career at Oxford except for a brief time at the University College in Cardiff. An authority on seventeenth-century England, he has published numerous studies, among which *Economic Problems of the Church* (1956), *Intellectual Origins of the English Revolution* (1965), and *God's Englishman* (1970) are noteworthy.

Editors:

JOHN W. BALDWIN is Professor of History at The Johns Hopkins University. Educated at Wheaton College (Illinois), The Pennsylvania State University, and Johns Hopkins, he taught at the University of

Michigan before returning to Hopkins. He is concerned with the intellectual and institutional history of the twelfth and thirteenth centuries and has published *The Medieval Theories of the Just Price* (1959), *Masters, Princes, and Merchants* (1970), and *The Scholastic Culture of the Middle Ages* (1971).

RICHARD A. GOLDTHWAITE is Associate Professor of History at The Johns Hopkins University. A graduate of Oberlin College and Columbia University, he taught at Kent State University before coming to Johns Hopkins. His scholarship in the social and economic history of the Italian Renaissance is represented by his book *Private Wealth in Renaissance Florence* (1968).

Index

Abelard, 4, 6, 7
Admonition to Parliament (1572), 115
Andrew of Brod, 101
Anglo-Burgundian government, 56, 57
Aquinas, Thomas, 7
Arras: conference at (1435), 57, 64, 65, n.48, 66
Azzo, 43, 44

Bacon, Nathaniel, 110
Barbarossa, Emperor Frederick, 30, 32
Barrow, Henry, 115
Basel, Council of (1431), 81
Beaupère, Jean, 53, 54, 77, n. 66
Bethlehem Chapel, Prague, 91
Biggs, Noah, 107,118
Bohaty, Nicholas, 102
Bologna: commune, 24, 25, 30, 31, 37-46
Bologna, University of, 4-6, 17-46;
academic lawyers and medieval empire, 26-37; alliance between student universities and the commune, 44, 45; communal regulation of professors, 41, 42; compared with University of Paris, 48; conflict between commune and student universities, 42, 43; conflict between doctors and student universities, 40; earliest organization of professors of law, 34; and emperors, 10, 11; enroachment of the commune on, 38; imperial privileges, 32-37; lawyers and the commune, 31, 32; legendary origins of, 43, 44; organization of students, 38; origins of, 19-25; professors and the commune, 44; public prestige of professors, 41,

42; relations between faculty and students, 40, 41; student universities and the *popolo*, 40
Bonaventure, 7
Boncompagno da Signa, 35, 41
Bourges, Council of, (1438), 68, n. 54
Bramhall, Bishop, 108
Brooke, Lord, 116
Browne, Robert, 115
Bunyan, John, 120
Burgundians, 49-58

Caen, University of, 57, 71
Calanchino, 39
Cambridge, University of, 7, 13, 119–26; vs. universities of Prague and Paris, 86
Canne, John, 116
Cauchon, Pierre, 53-55
Charles IV, King of Bohemia, 87, 88, 91
Charles VIII, King of France: and University of Paris, 58-72
Charlier, Gilles, 106
Chillenden, Edmund, 116
Christian of Prachatice, Master, 80, 106
Clarendon, Earl of, 131
Communes: origins of, 17-19; similarities to universities, 17-19
Conrad of Soltau, 89
Constance, Council of (1414), 86; and Hussite movement, 79ff.
Constance, Peace of, 30
Coppin, Richard, 116
Courcelles, Thomas de, 54, 57, 58
Crab, Roger, 116
Cromwell, Oliver, 109, 117–19

135

THE JOHNS HOPKINS UNIVERSITY PRESS

This book was composed in Baskerville text and display
by Baltimore Type and Composition Corporation. It was printed
on 55-lb. Sebago Antique by Universal Lithographers, Inc.
and bound in Holliston Roxite by L. H. Jenkins, Inc.